The Embodied Beloved
Honoring Your Whole Temple through Faith, Fitness and Nourishing Well
By De Bolton

The Embodied Beloved

HONORING YOUR WHOLE TEMPLE THROUGH MOVEMENT, NOURISHMENT AND MINDSET

De Bolton

© 2025 De Bolton. All rights reserved.

No part of this publication may be reproduced, stored in a retrieval system, or transmitted in any form or by any means electronic, mechanical, photocopying, recording, or otherwise—without the prior written permission of the publisher, except for brief quotations used in reviews or scholarly works.

The Embodied Beloved: Honoring your Whole Temple through Movement, Nourishment and Mindset.
By De Bolton

Scripture quotations are taken from the Holy Bible, New International Version® (NIV®), New King James Version® (NKJV), and other translations as noted. Used by permission. All rights reserved worldwide.

Published by De Bolton Enterprise
ISBN: 978-1-300-20013-0
First Edition: July, 2025

Cover and interior design by De Bolton

Printed in the United States of America

For permissions, speaking inquiries, or additional resources, visit:
www.faithfueledmom.com

This book is a work of non-fiction based on the author's personal experience and research. All medical or psychological insights are for educational purposes and should not replace professional advice.

To the One who loved me back to life
Jesus, my Healer, Redeemer, and Sustainer.
This is all for Your glory.

Acknowledgement

First, to God my Creator, my Redeemer, my Sustainer. This book would not exist without Your Spirit breathing it into being. You turned my pain into purpose, my striving into surrender, and my body into a temple that worships You. Thank You for loving me back to life.

To my family. Thank you for your patience, grace, and unconditional love. To my husband, my covering, my constant. Thank you for holding me steady when I wavered, for seeing the Beloved in me when I forgot who I was. Thank you for holding space for me to heal, dream, and become. Your unwavering love is a living example of Christ's tenderness. I wouldn't be here without your prayers, your patience, or your belief in me. You are my safe place and my greatest earthly gift.

To my daughters, you inspire every page. Watching you become who God made you to be has kept me grounded in mine and carrying a holy legacy.

To the brave women I've coached, cried with, prayed over, and learned from. The women who allowed me to witness their stories; clients, students, sisters in Christ. You gave language to what it means to live whole and free. Your courage, your honesty, and your hunger for healing are woven into every word. Your stories are etched on these pages. You showed me what embodied healing looks like.

To my mentors, coaches, and teachers who challenged me to keep growing, keep surrendering, and keep writing even when I doubted. Thank you for your wisdom and encouragement. You helped shape both this book and the woman who wrote it.

Finally, to you, Beloved reader, to every woman who has ever felt like her body was too much or not enough. You are not a burden. You are beloved. Thank you for trusting me with your time, your story, and your sacred body. May these pages point you back to the One who calls you whole, chosen, and dearly loved.

With deepest gratitude and awe,
  De Bolton

Table of Contents

Introduction
You Are the Embodied Beloved
Acknowledgement
Dear Beloved — 1
Part One: Awakening to Belovedness — 5-51
Chapter 1 – Becoming the Embodied Beloved *Embracing Your True Identity in Christ* — 6
Chapter 2 – Grace over Grind — 19
Choosing Rest, Not Relentless Hustle
Chapter 3 – Your Body Is a Temple — 30
Why Your Mind and Body Both Matter to God
Chapter 4 – Releasing False Scenarios — 43
How Trauma, Culture, and Lies Distort Our Self-View
Part Two: Healing and Restoration — 53-88
Chapter 5 – Forgiveness: The Doorway to Wholeness *Letting Go to Let God Heal* — 54
Chapter 6 – Living a Mindset of Freedom — 63
Walking in What's Already Been Given
Chapter 7 – The Gut–Heart–Brain Connection — 77
Embodied Emotions and the Path to Wholeness
Part Three: Reclaiming Movement — 89-165
Chapter 8 - Reclaiming Movement as a Spiritual Act — 0
Chapter 9 – Sustainable Fitness for Your Season *Grace-Based Strength and Stewardship* — 106
Chapter 10 – From Body Battle to Body Blessing *The Weight We Carry and How to Lay It Down* — 122

Chapter 11- What do I do to move? How much? How long? Why? *The Method of Movement that Matters*	136
Part Four: Nourishment and Freedom	147-210
Chapter 12-Nourish to Flourish *Rebuilding Your Relationship with Food*	148
Chapter 13 – Fed by Grace, Not by Guilt *Breaking Free from Diet Culture and Control*	158
Chapter 14 – Satisfy and Sustain *Eating with Peace, Presence, and Purpose*	172
Chapter 15– Holy Rhythms of Nourishment *Fasting, Feasting, and Living Restfully*	184
Chapter 16- What do I eat? How? Why?	199
Part Five: Whole Life Integration	211-248
Chapter 17 – Holy Habits, Not Hustle Routines	212
Chapter 18 – LivingWell, Living Whole *Sacred Rhythms for Mind, Body, and Spirit*	224
Chapter 19 – Making Disciples with Your Story *How Your Healing Becomes a Harvest*	235
Chapter 20 – My Body Story *An Invitation to Embody Your Own Redemption Narrative*	242
Epilogue	249
References	254

Author's Note: Before You Begin

I didn't write this book because I had everything figured out. I wrote it because I lived through the ache of not knowing who I was, the exhaustion of striving for worth, and the pain of being at war with my body.

For years, I believed I had to hustle for healing. That if I could lose the weight, follow the perfect plan, pray harder, or perform better, I would finally feel whole.

But what I discovered in the gym, in the kitchen, and on the floor in surrender was this:
Wholeness isn't earned.
It's received.
And it begins when you stop running and start returning.

This book is a collection of the truths that changed me. It's where theology meets embodiment, where Scripture and science converge, and where you'll find practices that don't just inform but transform. Because you weren't meant to live fragmented, spiritually awakened but emotionally numb, physically fit but disconnected from love. You were made to be whole.

Here, you'll be invited to reimagine health through the lens of belovedness.
To nourish your body without shame.
To move in freedom, not punishment.
To meet Jesus not just in your quiet time, but in your cravings, your fatigue, your breath, your bones.

So come as you are, no fixing required. Let the Spirit lead you into the sacred ground of your own body.

And may every page remind you:
You are not a problem to be solved.
You are the beloved, becoming whole.

With grace and grit,
De

Introduction: You Are Not Broken. You Are Becoming Whole.

There comes a moment when the mirror becomes more than glass.
It becomes a courtroom.
A confessional.
A place where you rehearse all the reasons you believe you're not enough.

Maybe you've stood there too pinching, covering, criticizing. Or maybe you've stopped looking altogether. Not because you don't care, but because you're tired of caring and never arriving.

I see you, Sis.

I was her too.

The girl who thought transformation meant shrinking herself. The woman who believed holiness meant hiding her body. The coach who told others how to be well while secretly feeling unworthy. But the gospel doesn't start with shame. It starts with love.

The truth is, God never asked us to be "fit enough" to be faithful. He called us *His* before we ever ran a mile, tracked a macro, or broke a generational cycle.

And yet, He also calls us to *honor* this body, this mind, this breath. To tend to the temple, not out of fear, but in reverent love.

This Book Is a Journey Back to Wholeness

The Embodied Beloved isn't a quick fix or a one-size-fits-all plan.
It's a slow return.
A sacred remembering.
A Spirit-led invitation to live like you're already loved, because you are.

You'll discover how:

- Scripture and neuroscience agree: your mind and body are deeply connected

- Movement can become worship, not punishment

- Nourishment can be sacred, not shameful

- Healing is a layered process not linear, but Spirit-led

- You are not just *saved* by grace, but *sustained* by it daily

What to Expect

Each chapter will guide you through:

- **The Beloved Speaks**: A real or composite story to remind you, you are not alone

- **Teaching**: Biblical truths and scientific insights to renew your mind

- **Selah Moment**: A breath prayer to help you pause and be present

- **Reflection Prompts**: Questions to help you go deeper in self-awareness and truth

- **Embodied Prayer**: A spiritual practice to bring the lesson into your body

- **Covered & Held Stillness**: Trauma-informed rest to meet your nervous system with grace

- **Movement-Based Practice**: Simple ways to reclaim strength and presence

You don't have to do this perfectly.
You just have to show up, willing to be loved into wholeness.

So take a breath.
Lay down the lie that your worth is found in a number, a plan, or your past.

You are already the Beloved.
Now, let's live like it one sacred step at a time.

Dear Beloved,

You were not meant to strive alone. You didn't find this book by accident.
Maybe you're weary from trying to "get it together." Maybe you've spent years chasing after discipline, a better body, or freedom in your health, only to end up exhausted, inconsistent, or ashamed. You know God wants more for you, but no matter how many times you start over, something inside still feels misaligned.

You are not broken.
You are beloved.

This book is not a plan to push you harder. It's an invitation to *come home to yourself*. The woman God designed before the world taught you to shrink, hustle, or hide.

You were created to live as the embodied beloved fully present in your body, anchored in grace, moving in freedom, and nourished from a place of love, not lack.

We live in a culture that promotes perfection, pressure, and performance. But the way of Jesus is different. He meets us in our humanity and says, "Come to me, all you who are weary and burdened, and I will give you rest."

Not *when you're consistent,*
Not *once you lose the weight,*
Not *after you fix your mindset.*

But now. As you are.

Over the next few chapters, you'll learn how to honor your whole temple, not just in theory but in your actual life. You'll discover how to:

- **Renew your mind** with truth and compassion
- **Move your body** with joy, intention, and worship
- **Nourish yourself** without shame, guilt, or obsession
- **Build sustainable habits** that support the life God is calling you to live

Not because you're chasing a version of who you think you *should* be, but because you're learning to live from who you *already are* in Christ.

I'm not here as an expert with all the answers. I'm here as a sister who knows what it's like to want healing and wholeness and to discover that it doesn't come from trying harder but from *receiving deeper.*

In this book, I will reveal my story and other Beloved Daughters of a Father who loves you so much that He wants to meet you where you are and take you further than any workout plan and meal plan can go. What you're about to experience isn't just another wellness plan. It's a transformation led by truth, compassion, and the Spirit of God Himself.

And transformation that lasts always begins with love.

You are invited.

Not just to read these words, but to wrestle with them, reflect on them, and respond with your whole being.

This book is your sacred space. A place to pause, to listen, to breathe, and to let the Holy Spirit speak to you not just through the pages of *The Embodied Beloved*, but through your own story, your body, and your becoming.

Here, you won't just *consume* truth you'll *engage* with it. You'll trace the fingerprints of God across your memories, your habits, your longings, and your beliefs. You'll release the narratives that no longer serve you and receive the ones rooted in grace, truth, and identity in Christ.

Each prompt, each breath prayer, each embodied practice is an invitation:
– To return to your body as a home, not a battleground.
– To reimagine your health as holy.
– To rewrite the story of what it means to be *well*.

You don't need to be perfect. You don't need to be ready. You just need to show up.

Bring your journal, your Bible, and your honest heart. Bring your joy, your questions, your resistance, your hope.

Let this be your altar and your sanctuary.
Because you, Beloved, are not just being changed you are being *formed*.

And transformation takes root when we pause long enough to notice it.

Let's begin one page at a time.

So take a deep breath.
Set down the pressure.

You don't need to fix yourself
You just need to return to the One who calls you beloved.

Let's begin.

With grace and expectancy,
De

Part 1: Awakening to Belovedness

Remembering Who You Are

Before you can transform your habits, you must be anchored in your identity.

This first part is about reclaiming the truth:
You are not broken beyond repair.
You are not an orphan striving for approval.
You are the Beloved called, chosen, and covered.

This is where sustainable transformation begins: not with a diet plan or a new routine, but with remembering who you already are in Christ.

Chapter 1: Becoming the Embodied Beloved

"He gathers the lambs in His arms and carries them close to His heart." — Isaiah 40:11

The Beloved Speaks

"For years, I believed I had to fix my body before I could be used by God. I was constantly starting over new programs, new diets, new shame. I loved Jesus, but I didn't love myself. I saw my body as a burden, not a blessing. And then, something shifted. I started showing up from love, not for it. I started moving to honor my temple, not to punish it. It wasn't a quick fix. It was slow, sacred healing. And for the first time in my life, I felt free in my body and close to God at the same time."
— The Beloved

I didn't always feel at home in my body. For most of my life, I carried the weight of shame, trauma, and disconnection not just in my heart, but in my hips, my stomach, and my shoulders. I learned to see my body as the enemy. A problem to solve. Something to control, shrink, silence, or ignore. I didn't know what it meant to live inside my body with love. I only knew what it felt like to live at war with it.

But something began to shift the moment I stopped seeing my body as a problem to fix and started seeing it as a temple to honor.

The phrase *embodied beloved* isn't just a poetic sentiment. It's your inheritance as a daughter of God. It's the truth about who you are, even if no one ever taught you to believe it. It's not about how much you weigh, how consistent you've been, or how much healing you've done. It's about how deeply you're willing to believe that you were made with care, purpose, and glory, and that your body isn't excluded from that truth.

To be the Embodied Beloved means you begin showing up from a place of truth, not performance. You stop striving to earn worth and start releasing the shame that's been wrapped around your size, your story, or your struggles. Slowly, gently, and with intention, you learn to trust your body again. And maybe for the first time, you start to believe that God didn't just make your soul good. He made your body good too. Embodiment is about presence. It's about coming home to yourself. Not as punishment, but as a promise. It's letting go of the pressure to perform and beginning to live in the fullness of who Christ already says you are.

Selah Moment: Breath Prayer

Use this space to pause and breathe truth into your body.

Inhale: *God, I honor my body.*
Exhale: *I am the Embodied Beloved.*

This process is not about perfection. It's not about flawless routines, spotless pasts, or checking every spiritual and physical box. It's about presence. Show up in the here and now, in your skin, in your story, with your soul fully engaged.

It's about tending to the parts of you that ache. It's about holding the pieces you were told didn't matter and honoring them with holy reverence.

Many of us have tried to patch emotional wounds with external fixes. We've mistaken body transformation for healing, thinking if we could just look "better," we would finally feel whole. But I've learned both personally and as a trainer. True freedom doesn't come from a smaller waistline. It comes from restoring the relationship you have with your own body.

I've watched clients follow the plan perfectly, achieve the look they were chasing, and still feel hollow. They're surprised that the same grief, shame, and heartbreak they carried before the transformation are still there. The pain never left. It just learned how to wear leggings.

The truth is, what they're longing for goes far deeper than a number on the scale. They're craving restoration. The kind that brings back what was lost: their voice, their confidence, and the freedom to walk into any room without shrinking. They want to feel without fear, to rest without guilt, to nourish themselves without shame, and to move in joy instead of punishment. And that kind of freedom? It doesn't come from a program. It comes from the healing that only Jesus can offer.

Your body is not the problem.
Your body is part of the promise.
The vessel that carries your calling.

The temple that holds your story.
The image-bearer that reflects God's glory.

The Bummer Lamb and the Orphan Spirit

Have you ever heard the story of a bummer lamb? It's a real thing in shepherding. Sometimes, a mother sheep will reject one of her lambs. The lamb isn't sick or wrong, but she refuses to nurse it or draw it near. Without help, the lamb won't survive not because of illness, but because of abandonment.

But when the shepherd sees it, he steps in. He wraps the lamb in cloth. He carries it close to his chest so it hears his heartbeat. He feeds it from a bottle, day and night. Eventually, when the lamb is strong enough, He brings it back to the flock.

That lamb grows up different, not weaker, but closer. Because it knows the shepherd's voice more intimately than the rest. It walks differently. It stays near. It trusts deeper.

That lamb… was me.
And maybe it's you, too.

"My sheep hear my voice. I know them. They follow me." John 10:27

I wasn't an orphan by circumstance, but I carried an orphan spirit for years. I lived like I had to earn love. I had to stay small to be safe. I had to fix myself to belong. Even in my faith, I was trying to impress a Father I didn't fully trust.

> *"I will not leave you as orphans; I will come to you."* — John 14:18

Jesus didn't just save my soul.
He rescued my story.
He picked up this bummer lamb and carried me close.

You are not a bummer lamb.
You are not forgotten.
You are not too much.
You are not alone.
You are the Embodied Beloved.
And He is your Shepherd.

This journey won't always be easy. There will be resistance, moments of deep emotion, and seasons when old wounds resurface. There will be tears you didn't expect and lies you'll have to confront and unlearn. But through it all, this process of coming home to your body, your truth, and your God-given worth will always be sacred.

When you move toward your body with compassion instead of contempt, you're not just making a wellness choice. You're making a worship choice.

> *"So here's what I want you to do, God helping you: Take your everyday, ordinary life, your sleeping, eating, going-to-work, and walking-around life, and place it before God as an offering. Embracing what God does for you is the best thing you can do for him. Don't become so well-adjusted to your culture that you fit into it without even thinking. Instead, fix your attention on God. You'll be changed from the inside out. Readily recognize what he wants from you, and quickly respond to it. Unlike the culture around you, always dragging you down to its level of immaturity, God brings the*

best out of you, develops well-formed maturity in you."
— Romans 12:1–2, The Message

Embodiment and the Wellness Journey

When I began my wellness journey, I thought the weight I wanted to lose was just physical. But it was emotional. Spiritual. Psychological. What I needed to shed couldn't be measured in pounds. It was patterns, narratives, fears, and trauma.

Everything changed when I realized embodiment wasn't just about being in shape.
It was about being present, spirit, soul, and body.

What Science Says About Being Embodied

In neuroscience and trauma research, *embodiment* refers to the integrated relationship between mind, body, and emotions. You don't just "have" a body, you *are* a body. According to Dr. Bessel van der Kolk, unprocessed trauma is not merely stored in the mind but shows up in the body itself as chronic tension, illness, emotional dysregulation, and pain (van der Kolk, 2014). Dr. Caroline Leaf reinforces this in *Switch on Your Brain*, teaching that our thoughts physically shape the brain. Through the process of neuroplasticity, intentional movement and mindful thought can literally rewire neural pathways toward healing (Leaf, 2013).

Another important component of embodiment is interoception. The awareness of your internal bodily states, like hunger, tension, or calm. Interoceptive awareness has been shown to directly support emotional regulation and trauma recovery. Studies reveal that increasing this type of awareness helps individuals reconnect with themselves and improves mental health outcomes (Price & Hooven, 2018).

Embodiment isn't just good science. It's good theology.

> *"You are fearfully and wonderfully made."* — Psalm 139:14

> *"Your body is a temple of the Holy Spirit."* — 1 Corinthians 6:19–20

> *"The Word became flesh and made His dwelling among us."* — John 1:14

> *"Offer your bodies as a living sacrifice… this is your spiritual worship."* — Romans 12:1

What the World Says, The Truth of God

The World says, the body stores trauma and emotions.

The Word says, *"A crushed spirit dries up the bones."* — Proverbs 17:22

The World says, The brain rewires through movement.

The Word says, *"In Him we live and move and have our being."* — Acts 17:28

The World says, Interoception fosters emotional healing.

The Word says, *"Be still and know that I am God."* — Psalm 46:10

The World says, The body is essential to restoration.

The Word says, *"Your body is a temple."* — 1 Corinthians 6:19

Being embodied means learning to listen to your body with compassion instead of criticism. It means honoring it as a sacred space. Where God dwells and speaks. It's allowing movement, breath, and presence to become part of your healing, your worship, and your daily rhythm with Him. Your body isn't in the way of your calling; it's part of the way God is calling you.

Reflection

1. What lies have you believed about your body that God never said?

2. In what ways have you tried to earn love, healing, or worth?

3. What would it look like to live like you are already the Beloved?

Embodied Prayer

Father God,
I release the shame I've carried in my body.
I let go of the belief that I have to earn your love or fix myself to be worthy. Thank You for creating me with intention, beauty, and purpose. Help me to live present in my body not to punish it, but to honor it.
Heal the orphan spirit in me.
Mark me with Your love.
Let me walk closely with Your voice like the bummer lambs You carry.
Teach me what it means to be the Embodied Beloved.

I receive this truth with open hands and a soft heart.
In Jesus' name, Amen.

Covered & Held Stillness Practice
Resting in the Shepherd's Arms
Setup:

- Find a quiet place to lie down, preferably on your back with a small blanket under your sacrum (tailbone area) for gentle elevation.

- Place one hand gently at the base of your skull, the other over your heart.

- Close your eyes.

Begin:
"Jesus, I am not a bummer lamb. I am not abandoned. I am carried. I am covered. I am held."

Breathe slowly and evenly.
Imagine the Shepherd gently lifting you, holding you against His chest, where you can hear the rhythm of His love.
With every breath in, receive His presence.
With every breath out, release the orphan spirit. Let it fall away.

Stay in stillness for 5–10 minutes.
When you feel ready, slowly bring your awareness back to your body and gently journal:

"What did my body say when I stopped to listen?"
"Where did I feel held?"

Movement-Based Exercise: Returning to the Temple

Walk the Promise

Setup:

This can be done indoors or outdoors, barefoot or in comfortable shoes.

Practice:
Begin walking slowly and mindfully.
With each step, repeat a truth out loud or in your spirit:

> Step 1: *"My body is not the problem."*
> Step 2: *"My body is part of the promise."*
> Step 3: *"I am not an orphan."*
> Step 4: *"I am the Beloved."*

Breathe in through your nose for 4 steps.
Exhale through your mouth for 4 steps.
Let your arms swing freely or place one hand over your heart as you walk.

Walk for 5–15 minutes. You can walk in silence, play gentle worship, or recite Psalm 23 aloud.

Optional Closing Practice:
Stand still, raise your arms overhead, and speak:

"I receive this temple. I reclaim this body. I return to the Shepherd who never lets go."

Ready to put what you've read into practice?
Download the FaithFueled Life App and take your journey deeper. Inside, you'll find guided breath prayers, embodied movement sessions, Scripture meditations, and soul-strengthening practices that bring this book to life. Whether you're seeking stillness, strength, or spiritual renewal, the app gives you real-time tools to embody your faith and steward your temple; anytime, anywhere.

Don't just read about transformation. Live it. www.tinyurl.com/FAITHFUELEDAPP and begin your journey of becoming the Embodied Beloved.

Chapter 2: Grace Over Grind

for anyone who enters God's rest also rests from their works,just as God did from his.
-Hebrews 4:10

The Beloved Speaks

"I thought being healthy meant being hard on myself. No days off. No slip-ups. I lived by food rules and scale numbers. If I missed a workout, I'd spiral. And still I felt empty. It wasn't until Coach De said, 'grace trains us' then something broke in me. I started slowing down, checking in with God, and showing up differently. I'm not perfect now but I'm peaceful. I don't hustle to be holy anymore. I move from rest. And that has changed everything."
— The Beloved

You weren't created to hustle your way into holiness. But somewhere along the way, many of us started believing that if we just worked harder, stayed disciplined, or pushed through the pain, then we'd finally be *enough*. We clung to the grind as proof of our worth spiritually, physically, emotionally.

The world calls it hustle culture. But in the Kingdom, hustle is just a baptized form of *striving*. And striving is the opposite of grace.

> *For it is by grace you have been saved, through faith—and this is not from yourselves, it is the gift of God— not by works, so that no one can boast.*
> — Ephesians 2:8–9 (NIV)

We live in a world that praises productivity and penalizes rest. Our culture glorifies pushing past limits, setting alarms for 5 a.m. workouts, and tracking every bite like it's a badge of honor. But behind the pursuit of "discipline" can be a deep fear of not measuring up, of losing control, of being unworthy.

Sometimes the hustle doesn't wear a suit and tie. It wears a fitness tracker and drinks protein shakes. It uses words like "clean," "willpower," and "dedication," while the heart beneath it whispers, "Maybe this will finally make me lovable."

But God never asked us to hustle our way into His presence. He never asked us to punish ourselves into health. He invited us to *abide*.

Shame, Striving, and the Nervous System

Dr. Curt Thompson, Christian psychiatrist and author of *The Soul of Shame*, teaches that shame is often the emotional engine of performance-based living. Shame convinces us we must *do* something to *be* someone.

> "Shame fuels the story that we must work harder, be more, do more to be loved, seen, and accepted."
> — *Dr. Curt Thompson*

Should
Have
Already
Mastered
Everything

From a neurological perspective, chronic striving activates the amygdala, the brain's threat detector. When we live in performance mode, our bodies stay locked in sympathetic nervous system dominance fight, flight, or freeze. We may appear "high achieving" on the outside, but inside, we're flooded with cortisol, inflammation, and low-level panic (Sapolsky, 2004).

Chronic stress from striving has been linked to anxiety, disordered eating, digestive problems, hormonal imbalances, and burnout (McEwen, 2006). When we grind without grace, our bodies bear the cost.

So what's the alternative?

Abide, Don't Strive

> *"Are you tired? Worn out? Burned out on religion? Come to me. Get away with me and you'll recover your life. I'll show you how to take a real rest. Walk with me and work with me—watch how I do it. Learn the unforced rhythms of grace. I won't lay anything heavy or ill-fitting on you. Keep company with me and you'll learn to live freely and lightly."*
> — Matthew 11:28–30 *(MSG)*

The invitation is clear: *real rest is found in Christ.* The Greek word used for *abide* in John 15 is menō meaning to remain, stay, dwell. It doesn't mean passive inactivity. It means *active connection.* You aren't giving up. You're *rooting down* into the One who grows fruit through you.

Striving says, "Try harder."
Abiding says, "Stay close."
Striving says, "Earn it."
Abiding says, "Receive it."

Striving says, "You're not doing enough."
Abiding says, "I'm already enough in Him."

Abiding is the holy rhythm of Kingdom wellness. Everything shifted in my walk with the Lord when the Holy Spirit gave me one word: Abide. At first, I didn't fully grasp it. I had heard it before, like many churchy words we tend to say without really understanding. But this time was different. The word stuck. It stirred something deeper in me.

So I opened my Bible to John 15:4 *"Remain in me, as I also remain in you."* And while I understood the basic idea, I stayed connected to Jesus. I felt the Spirit nudging me to go deeper. What did it *really* mean to abide? Was it just a feeling? A behavior? A mindset?

I began a journey of digging into Scripture and leaning into the Spirit. What I discovered surprised me. Abiding wasn't just about reading my Bible or praying more (though those are beautiful practices).

It was about *dependence.*

Delight.

Dwelling.

It meant learning to remain rooted when life felt unstable. To stay close when everything in me wanted to run, fix, or strive.

Take delight in the Lord, and he will give you the desires of your heart. Commit your way to the Lord; trust in him and he will do this: Psalm 37:4-5

I asked:
How do I abide when I feel anxious or disconnected?
Why is staying connected to the Vine so vital to my wellbeing spiritually, emotionally, and physically?
When do I tend to pull away?
And what would it cost me to remain instead of perform?

Over time, the Holy Spirit began to reveal the fruitlessness of my striving and the fruitfulness of staying. I didn't need to perform for God's presence. I needed to practice *remaining* in it.

And slowly, something changed.
Not overnight.
Not with a checklist.
But with daily moments of presence. Right where I was, not where I thought I should be.

Abiding became the way I returned to God not just in the quiet time, but in the chaos, the cravings, the carpool, the conflict. It wasn't about perfection. It was about *proximity*. Now, abiding isn't just a concept. It's my *compass*.

Wellness in the Kingdom Isn't Heavy
It's sacred.
It's sustainable.
It's full of grace.

> *"Christ has set us free to live a free life. So take your stand! Never again let anyone put a harness of slavery on you."*
> — *Galatians 5:1 (MSG)*

That includes the yoke of perfectionism. The burden of comparison. The weight of doing wellness "right" according to the world's standards. In the Kingdom, wellness isn't about reaching your "goal weight". It's about living from your *God-worth*.

Holiness was never supposed to feel like punishment. Healing was never supposed to feel like hustle. Grace unburdens the process and invites you to *walk in step with the Spirit* (Galatians 5:25).

Selah Moment: Breath Prayer

Breathe truth into your body and nervous system.

Inhale: I don't need to strive
Exhale: I am covered by His grace

This breath prayer is more than calming. It's *formational*. A study by Tindle et al. (2005) found that meditative prayer significantly lowered stress markers and improved mood regulation. Inhaling truth and exhaling peace helps anchor your nervous system in the presence of God.

Let breath become your bridge back to grace.

Grace Trains You, Not Guilt

Grace doesn't mean inaction. It means *intentional* action rooted in God's Spirit, not human effort.

> *"For the grace of God has appeared that offers salvation to all people.*
> *It teaches us to say 'No' to ungodliness and worldly passions,*
> *and to live self-controlled, upright and godly lives in this present age."*
> — *Titus 2:11–12 (NIV)*

Did you catch that?
Grace is a *teacher*.
It doesn't just forgive; it forms.
It doesn't just release; it *rebuilds*.
It trains our minds, our habits, and our health not with guilt, but with *gentle transformation*.

Dr. Dallas Willard once said:

> "Grace is not opposed to effort. It is opposed to *earning*."

This kind of effort flows from love, not lack.

This Is Grace in Action

Some days, grace leads you to lift heavy, fuel well, and show up in your strength. Other days, it looks like walking slowly with Jesus, crying in your car, or eating without judgment. Sometimes it's prepping healthy meals with intention. Other times it's eating what you have, sipping water, and letting that *be enough*.

Grace says: "You are never disqualified from my presence because of how you feel or what you ate."

Grace whispers: "Show up small if you must; just show up with Me."

This is not *laziness*.
This is *obedience*.
This is the holy rhythm of a life lived in sync with the Spirit.

> *"So whether you eat or drink or whatever you do, do it all for the glory of God."*
> — 1 Corinthians 10:31 (NIV)

Your Worth Was Never in the Hustle
Your healing was never in the grind.
Your holiness was never something you had to achieve.
It was *given*.
By *grace*.
Through *faith*.
Received in *love*.
Sustained by *presence*.

So, Beloved…
Let grace lead.
Let fruit grow in its time.
Let your body be a *temple* not a task.

Reflection Prompts
1. Where have you believed that "more effort" = "more holiness"?

2. What habits in your life feel more like striving than stewarding?

3. How can you shift one of your routines to align with *grace*, not *guilt*?

Embodied Prayer

Father,
I surrender the belief that I must earn health, earn healing, or earn Your love.
I release the hustle and receive Your grace.
Teach me what it means to live from rest not laziness, but holy rhythm.
Help me move, nourish, and renew not from pressure but from presence.
Thank You for Your light yoke.
Train me, Lord. I trust You.
In Jesus' name, Amen.

Covered & Held Stillness Practice

Lay Down the Hustle

Setup:

- Sit upright with your back supported, or lie on your back with your hands resting on your belly and heart.

- Keep your knees bent or legs supported comfort is the goal.

Begin:

> *"I do not earn grace. I receive it."*

Breathe in deeply. On your exhale, imagine laying down the burden of performance, perfection, and pressure.
With each breath, picture your nervous system settling your shoulders softening, your jaw unclenching, your chest opening.

As you rest, meditate on this truth:

> *"His yoke is easy and His burden is light"*
> *(Matthew 11:30).*

Stay in stillness for 3–5 minutes.
Let the breath remind your body: You are safe. You are enough. You are loved apart from your productivity.

Close with this whisper:

> *"Grace trains me not grind."*

Movement-Based Practice: Embodied Grace Flow

3-Minute Kneeling Reset

Setup:

- Begin on your knees (use a mat or folded blanket), toes untucked, spine tall.

Practice:

1. **Inhale:** Raise your arms slowly overhead

2. **Exhale:** Lower your arms slowly and bring palms together at heart center

3. **Repeat 3–5 cycles** while whispering or thinking:

   "Be still. Be loved. Be here."

4. **Optional Bow:**
   Lean forward into child's pose with arms stretched long.
   Let your forehead rest. Let your back release.
   Say: *"I am not my effort. I am His."*

   This short sequence can be done daily as a physical reminder to return to grace over grind.

Ready to put what you've read into practice?
Download the FaithFueled Life App and take your journey deeper. Inside, you'll find guided breath prayers, embodied movement sessions, Scripture meditations, and soul-strengthening practices that bring this book to life. Whether you're seeking stillness, strength, or spiritual renewal, the app gives you real-time tools to embody your faith and steward your temple; anytime, anywhere.

Don't just read about transformation. Live it.
www.tinyurl.com/FAITHFUELEDAPP and begin your journey of becoming the Embodied Beloved.

Chapter 3: Your Body Is a Temple, But So Is Your Mind

Do you not know that your bodies are temples of the Holy Spirit, who is in you, whom you have received from God? You are not your own; you were bought at a price. Therefore honor God with your bodies.
-1 Corinthians 6:19-20

The Beloved Speaks
"I used to think my body was the problem. But really, it was my mind. I believed I was too far gone, too inconsistent, too broken to change. I thought being harsh would fix me. But it only made me feel more disconnected from God, from myself, from my healing. Coach De taught me to renew my mind with truth daily, gently, intentionally has been the most powerful shift of all. Now, when I feel old thoughts creep in, I pause and speak Scripture instead. My temple isn't just what people see it's what I believe." — The Beloved

We've heard it before: *"Your body is a temple."* But what about your thoughts? What about your mind?

If your body is where the Spirit dwells, your mind is where the battle rages. And if we're going to honor our whole temple, we must begin with the sacred space between our ears. The stories, beliefs, memories, and thought patterns that either keep us stuck or set us free. When we are intentional about what we put in our mind it changes our decisions and direction.

The Battle of Belief: Mark 9 Commentary

When it comes to belief, I always think of the story of the demon-possessed boy. In Mark 9, a father brings his afflicted son to Jesus, and the encounter becomes a powerful picture of how belief intersects with healing. God's truth can reframe what we've believed about ourselves, our bodies, and our healing journey.

Let's walk through the passage together; with some reflections along the way.

> **Mark 9:17**
> *"Teacher, I brought you my son, who is possessed by a spirit that has robbed him of speech."*

(There are some things the enemy robs us from speaking about.)

> **Mark 9:18**
> *"Whenever it seizes him, it throws him to the ground. He foams at the mouth, gnashes his teeth, and becomes rigid."*

(There are things that have gotten stuck in our bodies, as we'll talk about soon. And how many times have emotions or past traumas knocked us down? Some of us are still living with rigid beliefs that are holding us back.)

> *"I asked your disciples to drive out the spirit, but they could not."*

(Some people have been disappointed by the church because they weren't able to help them.)

> **Mark 9:19**
> "You unbelieving generation,' Jesus replied, 'how long shall I stay with you? How long shall I put up with you? Bring the boy to me.'"

(Even after all the ways Jesus has shown up in our lives, there are still places we doubt He will heal, especially our bodies. And yet, He still chooses to be patient with us.)

> **Mark 9:20**
> "So they brought him. When the spirit saw Jesus, it immediately threw the boy into a convulsion."

(How many times does the enemy throw a tantrum the moment we start getting closer to Jesus? Raise your hand if you're currently experiencing an enemy tantrum because you've dared to press in deeper to Christ.)

> "He fell to the ground and rolled around, foaming at the mouth."

> **Mark 9:21-22**
> "Jesus asked the boy's father, 'How long has he been like this?'
> 'From childhood,' he answered. 'It has often thrown him into fire or water to kill him. But if you can do anything, take pity on us and help us.'"

(There are traumas you've been carrying since childhood. Experiences that still try to drown you or burn you alive emotionally. And maybe like this father, you've whispered, "If you can help, Jesus...")

Mark 9:23
"'If you can'?" said Jesus. "Everything is possible for one who believes."

Mark 9:24
"Immediately the boy's father exclaimed, 'I do believe; help me overcome my unbelief!'"

(I don't know about you, but I've walked through seasons where I believed God could heal others, but I wasn't sure He'd do it for me. Or I knew healing was possible, but my past made me question whether it was possible for me. That's where surrender begins. And sometimes, we need someone to walk with us through it.)

Mark 9:25
"When Jesus saw that a crowd was running to the scene, he rebuked the impure spirit. 'You deaf and mute spirit,' he said, 'I command you, come out of him and never enter him again.'"

(This is a spirit that is unheard and unseen. Kind of like the negative self-talk running through your mind that no one else can hear but you. That narrative is real. And it needs to go.)

Mark 9:26
"The spirit shrieked, convulsed him violently and came out. The boy looked so much like a corpse that many said, 'He's dead.'"

(That's deliverance. And sometimes, deliverance doesn't look gentle. It can feel violent. It shakes things loose. It looks messy. Healing from trauma can feel like a part of you is dying so something new can live. And yet...)

> **Mark 9:27**
> "But Jesus took him by the hand and lifted him to his feet, and he stood up."

(That's Jesus. He lifts us up. When everyone else says, "She's done," He says, "Get up, Daughter.")

> **Mark 9:28-29**
> "After Jesus had gone indoors, his disciples asked him privately, 'Why couldn't we drive it out?' He replied, 'This kind can come out only by prayer.'"(Some translations have: "and fasting.")
>
> We'll talk about the significance of fasting in future chapters.

What This Means for You
Belief is transformational and powerful.
It wasn't until Abraham believed, as Romans 4 reminds us, that he received the promises of God.

Your beliefs will either transform you or trap you. They will either set you free or keep you stuck in the fire or under the water.

Your beliefs are your internal GPS.
Every action, every decision, every reaction flows from what you believe deep down.

Some of those beliefs were never yours to carry.
Some are drowning you.
Some are burning you.

But healing comes when you bring them to Jesus. And for some of us, those strongholds can only be broken through intentional forgiveness, releasing and rewiring thought processes.

There is deliverance. There is healing. And it comes from getting closer to Jesus through fasting, prayer, and surrender.

The Power of Belief & the Science of Neuroplasticity

Modern neuroscience affirms what Scripture has long said: transformation begins in the mind. The term *neuroplasticity* refers to the brain's ability to rewire itself based on thought patterns, behaviors, and emotional experiences. What we meditate on, we strengthen. In other words what we repeat takes root.

> *"As someone thinks within himself, so he is."*
> (Proverbs 23:7, NASB)

Dr. Caroline Leaf, a cognitive neuroscientist, writes:

> "Thoughts are real, physical things that occupy mental real estate. Every time you have a thought, it sets off a cascade of electrical and chemical responses in your brain, which in turn shape your brain's structure and function."
> —*Switch On Your Brain* (2013)

Our beliefs are not passive. They are powerful. They activate neural pathways that reinforce our perception of self, God, and others. Just as trauma rewires the brain toward hypervigilance and fear, healing rewires it toward safety, presence, and peace.

And Scripture calls us into this renewal:

> *"And do not be conformed to this world, but be transformed by the renewing of your mind, so that you may prove what the will of God is, that which is good and acceptable and perfect."* (Romans 12:2, NASB)

Not conformed. Not conditioned. But transformed. Not once, but again and again. This is a lot to process. Let's take a pause and breath.

Selah Moment: Breath Prayer

Inhale: *"You have given me a sound mind..."*
Exhale: *"...and I surrender every thought to You."*

Take a few slow breaths. Let the tension in your shoulders fall. Let the critical inner voice fade into stillness. Let the lies lose their grip as you breathe in truth.

Now, imagine the temple of your mind once cluttered
with fear, shame, and perfectionism
being swept clean by the gentle hand of Jesus.

Picture Him flipping the tables.
Not out of anger, but with holy love.
Because you are a sacred space.
Because your thoughts matter to Him.

Ask Him:
What lies have I been living under?
What truth do You want to plant here instead?

Stay here. Breathe.
Let your thoughts be rewired by love.

The Temple Within the Temple
1 Corinthians 6:19–20 (NIV) says:
Do you not know that your bodies are temples of the Holy Spirit, who is in you, whom you have received from God? You are not your own; you were bought at a price. Therefore, honor God with your bodies.

Your body is a sacred dwelling. It is the inhabitant of the Holy Spirit who is part of the trinity and out of anywhere it can take up residence. You beloved are the choice without a doubt. Just as you are. But we can't stop there.

Romans 12:2 (NIV) adds:
"Do not conform to the pattern of this world, but be transformed

by the renewing of your mind. Then you will be able to test and approve what God's will is—his good, pleasing, and perfect will."

Your mind is not just a thought center. It's a temple within the temple. And like any temple, it needs tending.
Clearing.
Renewal.
Consecration.

We can't designate only part of the temple. It's a whole.

Where Trauma and Thought Patterns Live

Trauma, shame, and unhealed beliefs often live in the body-mind connection of the Spirit dwellings.

You may feel them as:

- Constant fatigue, even after rest
- Sudden anxiety or emotional eating
- Body tension in your shoulders, gut, or chest
- Critical inner talk that sounds strangely familiar

That's because the body stores what the mind can't process. And the mind replays what the body still remembers.

This is why *fitness without renewal* doesn't bring freedom.
This is why *diets without healing* don't last.
This is why *prayer without transformation* often feels like defeat.

You were never meant to separate the two. You are an integrated being, just like your Father with the body, mind, and spirit. And wholeness requires tending to all of you.

Cleaning Out the Mental Temple

Jesus didn't just teach in temples. He cleansed them. In Matthew 21:12–13, He flipped tables and cleared out what didn't belong. Not out of anger, but out of righteous love for sacred space.

"It is written," he said to them, "'My house will be called a house of prayer,' but you are making it 'a den of robbers. Matthew 21:13

We are being robbed of the fullness of being with our Fathers because we are lying and cheating on ourselves. Sometimes, He wants to do the same in our minds.

Not with shame.
Not with judgment.
But with gentle authority and healing power.

God wants to gently but powerfully clear out the lies that have shaped how you see yourself. Those false narratives that whisper you're not enough unless you shrink, strive, or prove your worth.

He's ready to flip the tables on the toxic patterns of perfectionism, body shame, and diet culture that have taken up space in your heart like unwelcome guests. And in their place, He wants to restore your thought life. Replacing anxiety with peace, confusion with clarity, and self-condemnation with the truth of who you are in Him: beloved, chosen, and whole.

Renewal Is an Ongoing Process

It's not a one-time fix but a daily rhythm of care and attention. You find yourself off beat sometimes, but when you come to

Jesus, you can get back to the rhythms of grace. By taking the burdens to Him. (Matthew 11:28-31)

Renewing your mind is much like nourishing your body. Each day, you learn to recognize the lies that try to take root and intentionally replace them with the truth of God's Word. You begin to notice the patterns. Those old mental ruts of fear, shame, or unworthiness, and gently interrupt them with grace. Instead of reacting with harsh self-criticism, you meet the moment with kindness, honoring the process of transformation as holy, slow, and Spirit-led. It's not about "positive thinking." It's about biblical thinking.

Reflection Prompts:
1. What "thought clutter" has been taking up sacred space in your mind?
2. Are there phrases or patterns you need to surrender to Jesus?
3. What might it look like to allow God to "flip the tables" in your mind today?
4. What new thought or truth do you want to begin practicing?

Embodied Prayer:
Father God,
Come into the temple of my mind and make it holy again.
Flip the tables of fear, doubt, shame, and comparison.
Cleanse the space I've allowed to be filled with clutter.
Help me take every thought captive and make it obedient to You.
Let my mind be a place of peace, renewal, and truth.
Thank You for making all things, including my thoughts, new.
In Your name, Amen.

Covered & Held Stillness Practice

The Renewing Rest

Setup:

- Lie flat on your back or recline with your head supported.

- Place one hand on your forehead (symbolizing your thoughts) and the other on your belly (symbolizing your center).

Begin:
Breathe slowly and deeply.
As you inhale, say silently: *"Renew my mind."*
As you exhale, say: *"Bring peace to my body."*

Allow yourself to rest in God's presence, no striving, no fixing. Imagine the lies you've believed about your worth, your body, and your past being gently washed away with each breath.

Invite the Holy Spirit to highlight just one truth He wants you to carry forward.

> *"Do not conform to the pattern of this world, but be transformed by the renewing of your mind."*
> — Romans 12:2

Close by whispering:

> *"I am not what I think. I am who God says I am."*

Movement-Based Practice: Reclaim the Narrative

Rise & Declare

Setup:
Stand tall with feet grounded and knees slightly soft.
You may want to do this in front of a mirror, or with your eyes closed in a quiet space.

Practice:

1. **Raise your arms slowly overhead**, stretch through your fingers.
   Say aloud or think: *"My body is a temple."*

2. **Lower your hands to your heart**, palms together.
   Say: *"My mind is being renewed."*

3. **Place both hands over your head**, then let them fall open.
   Say: *"I release false narratives."*

Repeat the full cycle 3–5 times. Move slowly. Let the movements reflect surrender and strength.

Optional Scripture declaration to speak aloud as you move:

> *"I have the mind of Christ."* — 1 Corinthians 2:16

Chapter 4: Releasing False Scenarios

"He has sent me to bind up the brokenhearted, to proclaim freedom for the captives and release from darkness for the prisoners." -Isaiah 61:1(NIV)

The Beloved Speaks

"I learned to wear masks before I even knew what my real face looked like. I became the overachiever, the peacemaker, the strong Black woman who could handle anything, because that's what was expected. That's how I stayed safe. But when I finally slowed down, the silence was deafening. Who am I if I'm not performing? What happens if I stop proving? That's when I realized. I wasn't living in God's truth. I was living in a tangled web of cluttered narratives that were never mine to carry."- The Beloved

We are all shaped by stories. But not all stories tell the truth. Some of the loudest messages that form our identity don't come from God. They come from trauma, culture, or the expectations of others. They arrive subtly, quietly. A raised eyebrow. A parent's absence. A pastor's silence. A comment about your body. Praise for your hustle. And slowly, your identity gets shaped not by who you are in Christ, but by what you learned you must be to survive.

These internalized stories are what I call *scenarios that take root* in the nervous system and become embodied. They tell us:

- "You have to be perfect to be loved."
- "You're too much. Tone it down."
- "If you don't do it all, everything will fall apart."
- "Be grateful, don't need too much."
- "Your body is a problem to fix, not a temple to honor."

But these are lies. They may feel *true* because they are familiar. They may even be generational, passed down through silence and survival. But they are not the *truth*. And until we name and release them, they will continue to distort how we see ourselves and how we live in our bodies.

Selah Moment: Breath Prayer

Inhale: "Jesus, clear the clutter."
Exhale: "Anchor me in Your truth."

Repeat slowly for 2–3 minutes, allowing space between breaths.

How Clutter Becomes a Story in the Body

The stories we carry are not just in our minds. They live in our muscles, our breath, our blood. Long before a thought becomes a belief, and long before a belief becomes a behavior, it takes root somewhere in the body. The tension you feel in your shoulders. The gut reaction that twists before you speak. The tight jaw you clench without realizing it. These aren't just quirks of posture or habit. They are signposts. Your body is telling a story it was never meant to carry alone.

Science is only now catching up to what God has always known: trauma leaves an imprint, not just on our memory, but on our biology.

Neuroscience reveals that when we rehearse certain thoughts, especially ones tethered to fear, shame, or unworthiness. We strengthen neural pathways in the brain (Leaf, 2020). These pathways become our default settings. Like well-worn trails, they shape our responses to the world. We react before we reason. We anticipate rejection. We expect chaos. And even when our circumstances change, those mental grooves remain until they are intentionally rewired through new patterns of safety, presence, and truth.

Epigenetics confirms that trauma is not only personal, it's generational. Research shows that unhealed pain can alter gene expression, affecting how we regulate stress, emotion, and even how we hold ourselves physically (Yehuda & Lehrner, 2018). This means some of the survival instincts we carry didn't start with us. They were passed down. Inherited. Woven into our stories before we ever had words. Our very posture, rounded shoulders, shallow breath, and turned-in knees can reflect a lineage of loss.

Somatic psychology echoes this truth: the body remembers what the mind forgets. When wounds go unprocessed, they don't disappear; they go underground. Into the fascia. Into the nervous system. Into the tension patterns and chronic conditions we normalize. We learn to adapt to pain rather than address it. We hustle through heartache instead of healing it.

But that emotional clutter doesn't disappear. It simply finds a home in the body.

And yet, God has been saying this all along.

> *"The Lord, the compassionate and gracious God, slow to anger, abounding in love and faithfulness... Yet He does not leave the guilty unpunished; He punishes the children and their children for the sin of the parents to the third and fourth generation."*
> — Exodus 34:6–7 (NIV)

This passage isn't just about judgment. It's about consequences woven into creation. Unrepented sin and unhealed trauma can echo across generations. But even here, the mercy of God shines brighter. Just a few chapters later, we're told His love extends "to a thousand generations of those who love Him and keep His commandments" (Deuteronomy 7:9). Trauma may echo, but mercy resounds louder.

This is the divine paradox of being embodied: our pain may have roots deeper than we knew, but healing can reach even deeper. What has been passed down can be uprooted. What has been stored can be surrendered. God doesn't just redeem your story. He rewrites it in your very cells.

Beloved, you are not stuck in the cycle. You are not doomed to repeat the past. Through Jesus, you carry not only the memory of pain but the possibility of resurrection. The clutter in your body isn't a curse. It's an invitation. To listen. To process. To surrender. And to let God transform every thread of your embodied story into something whole, holy, and healed.

God's Narrative vs. the Enemy's Lies

There's a war for your narrative. And it doesn't just live in the spiritual realm. It echoes in your mind, pulses through your body, and affects every decision you make. Scripture tells us that the enemy is the "father of lies" (John 8:44), which means deception is his native language. But here's what we sometimes miss: the lies don't always sound loud. Sometimes, they sound *familiar*. Sometimes, they sound like our own voice.

God speaks identity. *You are My beloved daughter, in whom I am well pleased.*
The enemy counters with insecurity. *Who do you think you are? You're not enough.* God declares love. *Nothing can separate you from my love.* The enemy whispers shame. *If they really knew you, they'd walk away.*

This is the strategy of spiritual warfare: not always dramatic, but always destructive. The enemy doesn't need to steal your future if he can confuse your identity. He doesn't need to chain your body if he can clutter your beliefs.

And the battlefield? It's your agreement. Every time we choose to believe the lie. *I'm too much, I'll never change, my body is a burden.* We strengthen a false narrative in our neurobiology. Neural pathways influence not just how we think, but how we feel and move in the world. The more we meditate on lies, the more they become our lived experience. Shame gets stored in our nervous system. Insecurity shapes our posture. Fear becomes the filter through which we perceive God, others, and ourselves.

But Beloved, you were not created to live by fictitious scenarios. You were created to live by the Word made flesh. The One who spoke the stars into existence and also speaks *your name with delight.*

It's time to break the agreement. It's time to untangle yourself from the lies that have rooted in your nervous system and reclaim the narrative God wrote over your life before your first breath.

> "*Before I formed you in the womb, I knew you*" (Jeremiah 1:5).

> "*You are God's workmanship, created in Christ Jesus to do good works*" (Ephesians 2:10).

Decluttering your inner narrative is not about striving for positivity. It's about *repentance*. Turning away from lies and realigning with truth. It's spiritual, it's neurological, and it's deeply embodied.

You may feel the effects of those false agreements in your body tight chest, fatigue, emotional eating, and self-criticism. But the good news is, through the renewing of your mind (Romans 12:2), and by the power of the Holy Spirit, you can *rewire the story.*

You can choose to agree with God's voice.
You can trade insecurity for inheritance.
Shame for sonship.
Fear for faith.

This is not just mindset work. It's heart, soul, and body restoration.

You are not too broken.
You are not too far gone.
You are not what happened to you.
You are who God says you are.

His narrative is the only one that leads to healing, freedom, and embodied wholeness.

Reflection Prompts
Take a deep breath. Pause. Be honest.

1. What are the recurring thoughts you believe about yourself that don't align with God's Word?

2. Where do you think those beliefs came from: family, trauma, culture, or church?

3. How do those beliefs show up in your body? Your posture? Your habits? Your relationships?

4. What new narrative is God offering you in this season?

Embodied Prayer
Place one hand over your heart, the other on your belly. Close your eyes.
Speak this aloud to yourself:

"Father God,
I release the stories that are not mine to carry.
I break the agreement with lies spoken over me.
I am not my trauma. I am not what culture demands.
I am Yours, God. Fully loved. Fully seen. Fully known. In Jesus' name, Amen.

Now gently stretch your arms wide in surrender.
Lift your chest. Unclench your jaw. Let your belly soften.
Stay here. Just breathe.

Covered & Held Stillness Practice
Somatic Visualization: The Story Table

1. Sit comfortably or lie on your back with one hand on your heart.

2. Imagine Jesus seated at a large table, inviting you to lay your stories before Him.

3. See yourself placing each one on the table: the labels, the pressure, the pain.

4. One by one, as you release them, feel your body lighten.

5. When the table is full, hear Jesus say: *"Let me rewrite your story."*

Stay in this stillness for 5–7 minutes, resting in the presence of the One who calls you Beloved.

Movement Practice: Untangling the Lies

This practice invites release through movement:

1. **Spinal Rolls** – From a standing position, gently roll down and up, releasing tension from head to tailbone.

2. **Hip Circles** – Hands on hips, make wide circles to mobilize and release stored emotion.

3. **Shoulder Rolls + Arm Sweeps** – Big sweeping movements to open the chest and shake off pressure.

4. **Grounding Steps–** Walk slowly in place or around the room, speaking truth aloud:
    - "I am not what I do."
    - "I am not what happened to me."
    - "I am a daughter of the King."

End by placing your hands on your belly and heart again, saying: *"I am home in God's truth*

Ready to put what you've read into practice?
Download the FaithFueled Life App and take your journey deeper. Inside, you'll find guided breath prayers, embodied movement sessions, Scripture meditations, and soul-strengthening practices that bring this book to life. Whether you're seeking stillness, strength, or spiritual renewal, the app gives you real-time tools to embody your faith and steward your temple—anytime, anywhere.

Don't just read about transformation. Live it.
www.tinyurl.com/FAITHFUELEDAPP and begin your journey of becoming the Embodied Beloved.

Part 2: Renewal of Mind and Body

Healing the Stories You Carry

Lasting change is not behavior modification.
It is heart transformation, and it starts in your beliefs.

Here we explore the intersection of neuroscience, trauma recovery, and Scripture, uncovering the hidden narratives that have shaped how you view your body, food, and worth.

Renewing your mind is not a one-time event. It is a daily invitation into freedom.

Chapter 5: Forgiveness: The Doorway to Wholeness

"Bear with each other and forgive one another if any of you has a grievance against someone. Forgive as the Lord forgave you."
— Colossians 3:13 (NIV)

The Beloved Speaks

"I was doing all the right things, eating better, exercising, even reading my Bible, but I still felt stuck. I didn't realize I was holding onto so much unforgiveness. Toward others. Toward my past. Toward myself. I thought discipline would heal me. But it was forgiveness that set me free. The moment I released what I'd been carrying, everything softened. I stopped punishing my body. I stopped believing I had to earn healing. Forgiveness made room for joy again. For peace. For breath."
— The Beloved

There is no true wellness without forgiveness.
Because healing doesn't happen in a body held hostage by bitterness. I hold space for small group coaching and personal coaching and many of my clients cannot move forward without forgiveness. Forgiving others or forgiving themselves both are challenging, but forgiving themselves seems to be the hardest for most. And forgiveness isn't a one time fix like most of the tools you will find in this book it is an ongoing practice.

Unforgiveness doesn't just weigh on your heart. It shows up in your body.
In your posture.
Your digestion.
Your breath.
Your immune system.
Your nervous system.

It roots into your biology like a parasite, draining life from places meant to flourish. Forgiveness, however, is not just a spiritual principle; it's a physiological release. It's a divine invitation to return your mind, body, and spirit to peace.

What Forgiveness Really Is
Let's be clear, forgiveness is not permission, and neither is grace.
It does not excuse what happened.
It does not require reconciliation.
It does not deny pain.
It does not forget.

Forgiveness says:
"I'm not going to carry this anymore."
"I'm not going to let this moment define my whole body."
"I choose freedom over resentment."

It's an act of radical grace.
Not for the person who hurt you; but for the healing God wants to release in you.

Selah Moment: Breath Prayer

Use this space to pause and breathe truth into your body.

Inhale: "I release what doesn't serve me."
Exhale: "I am forgiven and free."

Forgiveness and the Body

This is the sacred paradox of being embodied: unforgiveness doesn't just sit in our minds. It settles into our bodies, trapping us in survival mode. When we hold onto bitterness, our bodies pay the price. Dr. Everett Worthington, a leading voice in forgiveness therapy, explains that unresolved resentment keeps us locked in chronic stress, constantly flooding our system with cortisol and weakening the immune response (Worthington & Scherer, 2004).

It's not just emotional, it's cellular. Trauma researcher Dr. Bessel van der Kolk shows that painful memories don't stay neatly filed away in our thoughts; they embed themselves into our tissues and nervous systems, impacting how we move, breathe, and feel (van der Kolk, 2014).

But the good news? Forgiveness doesn't just change your heart. It can literally change your brain. Dr. Caroline Leaf teaches that choosing to forgive reshapes neural pathways, reducing inflammation and helping restore mental clarity (Leaf, 2013).

When we forgive, it's as if the entire body exhales. The nervous system often braced in silent tension begins to soften. Cortisol, that relentless messenger of stress and self-preservation, retreats. The gut, which quietly stores so much unprocessed emotion, begins to move in harmony again. The immune system, once weighed down by internal conflict, begins the work of rebuilding. Even our breath shifts no longer short and shallow, but slow and steady, like a soul coming home.

Forgiveness doesn't erase the pain. It doesn't deny what was done. But it does release your whole being from the weight of carrying it. In the end, it's not just an act of mercy toward another, it's an act of profound healing for yourself.

Jesus and the Model of Forgiveness

On the cross, Jesus modeled the ultimate act of forgiveness:

> *"Father, forgive them, for they do not know what they are doing."* — Luke 23:34 (NIV)

Jesus didn't wait for an apology. He didn't require full understanding. He forgave in the middle of the wounding. Forgiveness, He showed us, is always upstream of healing. It's the river that clears the debris of bitterness before it can harden into bondage.

When Jesus told His followers to forgive seventy times seven times (Matthew 18:21–22), it wasn't because forgiveness is easy. It was because forgiveness is necessary for freedom. It takes practice and consistent effort. "Everytime you remember it you have to forgive again."

The Kingdom of God is not founded on grudges; it is built on grace. When we withhold forgiveness, we don't just bind others, we imprison ourselves. Forgiveness, even when the wound is still raw, is a choice: the choice to walk in life, to step into freedom, to move toward wholeness. It is the way of

Christ, the true reflection of His image in us. Often, it's the very thing standing between us and the lasting freedom we long for.

> "Bear with each other and forgive one another if any of you has a grievance against someone. Forgive as the Lord forgave you." — Colossians 3:13 (NIV)

> "Blessed is the one whose transgressions are forgiven, whose sins are covered." — Psalm 32:1 (NIV)

What About Self-Forgiveness?

This is where many of us stay stuck: we know God has forgiven us. We may have even extended forgiveness to others. But when it comes to ourselves; our past, our mistakes, our bodies we hesitate. We brace. We believe that if we forgive ourselves, we're somehow letting ourselves off the hook. But let me say this with grace and clarity: forgiving yourself is not selfish, it's sacred.

It's not an act of erasing the past, but of releasing its hold over your present. Forgiveness isn't saying "it didn't matter." It's saying, "Jesus already paid for this." It's standing in agreement with the cross. You are not your past. You are not your failures. You are not the sum of your coping mechanisms. You are the Beloved covered, redeemed, and being made whole.

The Lord Himself says, *"I, even I, am He who blots out your transgressions, for My own sake, and remembers your sins no more"* (Isaiah 43:25, NIV). When we forgive ourselves, we join God in remembering no more not by forgetting what happened, but by refusing to be ruled by it. This is not denial. This is deliverance.

And it's not just your spirit that's released in forgiveness, your body is too. Studies have shown that people who practice forgiveness experience lower levels of anxiety, depression, and anger, as well as improved immune function and heart health (Toussaint et al., 2016). Forgiveness literally changes your biology. When you let go of what's been chaining your heart, your body begins to heal as well.

So breathe this in: You are not what you've done. You are not what's been done to you.
You are the Beloved.
And you are already forgiven.

Forgiveness in the Body: A Gentle Practice

Try this simple practice when unforgiveness feels stored in your body:

1. **Place one hand on your chest. One on your belly.**

2. **Breathe in deeply.**
   Say silently: *"I release the need to carry this alone."*

3. **Exhale slowly.**
   Say: *"I choose freedom. I choose grace."*

4. **Name what you're holding.**
   You don't need to fix it just name it.

5. **Surrender it to Jesus.**
   Say: *"This doesn't belong to me anymore."*

Do this as often as needed.
Forgiveness is not a one-time event.
It's a process of releasing layer by layer. Until your body becomes light again.

Reflection Prompts

1. Who have I not forgiven, and what is it costing my body?

2. What am I still holding against myself that Jesus has already covered?

3. What would freedom feel like in my body if I fully forgave?

Embodied Prayer

Jesus,
You forgave while You were still being wounded.
You didn't wait for perfection. You chose mercy.
I want to live like that.
But I confess I've been holding on to hurt.
I've been carrying pain, resentment, and guilt in my body, and I'm tired.
I lay it at Your feet now.
I choose to forgive the ones who hurt me.
I choose to forgive myself for what I didn't know, couldn't change, or didn't do.
I release the grip of shame and welcome Your peace.
Thank You for carrying what I no longer have to.
Teach me to walk in the lightness of grace.
In Your name, Amen.

Covered & Held Stillness Practice
Setup:

Sit comfortably or lie down in stillness.

Place your hands palm-up over your lap or resting over your heart and belly.

Begin:

Breathe in deeply through your nose.

As you exhale, whisper or think: "I let it go."

Picture the heaviness of resentment, self-blame, or betrayal falling off of your shoulders, hips, and chest.

Feel the ground holding you as God holds your story.

You don't have to figure out how to forgive fully. You just have to be willing.

Visualize the weight of unforgiveness as a heavy cloak sliding off your back.

"Come to Me, all who are weary and burdened, and I will give you rest." — Matthew 11:28

Close by saying:

"Jesus, I release what was never mine to carry."

Rest here as long as needed.

Movement-Based Exercise: Forgiveness Flow
Setup:
Stand in a grounded stance. Feet hip-width apart, soft knees, relaxed arms.

Practice:

1. Begin by gently shaking out your hands, arms, and shoulders.

Let it be messy, loose, unstructured. This isn't performance; it's release.

Say: "I don't need to hold this anymore."

2. Bring your arms overhead in a big inhale, reaching tall.

3. Exhale as you sweep your arms down and bow slightly, like laying something at Jesus' feet.

Say: "I lay it down."

4. Repeat 3–5 times, visualizing the names, memories, or burdens you are surrendering with each movement.

5. End by standing still, placing one hand over your heart and one over your belly.

Say: "I am free. I am forgiven. I am the Beloved."

Chapter 6: Living a Mindset of Freedom

"Where the Spirit of the Lord is, there is freedom."-
2 Corinthians 3:17

The Beloved Speaks

"I didn't know I was living in a mental prison until I started to taste freedom. I used to obsess over every bite, every step, every failure. If I wasn't doing it perfectly, I felt like I wasn't doing it at all. But then Coach De reminded me of the truth: I'm already free. I just have to live like it. That truth started to shape how I think. Now I make decisions from freedom, not fear. I don't strive, I surrender. And somehow, that's what brought me the consistency I'd been chasing."
— The Beloved

Some prisons don't come with bars or barbed wire. They are built silently, cell by cell, in the hidden places of our minds. Many of us live behind these invisible walls for years, sometimes decades, shaped by internal scripts we never chose but learned to recite:

"You are only as good as your performance."
"You are only worthy if you succeed."
"You are only lovable if you get it right."

These beliefs don't just shape our thoughts. They shape our bodies. They tighten our shoulders, shallow our breath, and constrict our capacity to receive love.

As a trauma-informed Christian Holistic Health practitioner, I've worked with women from all walks of life. Some in the boardroom, some in the gym, and others behind the concrete walls of correctional facilities. And I've come to see this truth: we are all fighting for freedom. Some are bound by bars, and some by beliefs. Some wear uniforms that mark their sentence; others wear smiles that mask their pain. But bondage is bondage, whether seen or unseen. And every woman I've served, regardless of her location, carries a sacred story worth honoring.

Freedom is not found in the absence of struggle. It's found in the presence of truth.

Jesus said, *"You will know the truth, and the truth will set you free"* (John 8:32, NIV).

He wasn't just speaking of theological knowledge. He was pointing us to a deeper encounter with the living, breathing Word who renews our minds and rewrites our stories. Our brains are not fixed. Through neuroplasticity, the same thoughts that once kept us imprisoned can, through repeated truth and loving presence, become pathways to peace and freedom.

This is the surrendered work of embodiment. Not just knowing we're free in Christ, but learning to live free in our skin. To move in a way that says,

"I am not what I've done, I am not what's been done to me. I am the Beloved."

Whether I'm guiding a woman through gentle movement in a prison gymnasium or holding space for a client learning to breathe deeply for the first time in decades, the invitation is the same: come out of hiding. You are not too far gone. You are not disqualified. You are deeply known, fully seen, and still chosen. Freedom is not reserved for the few. It is the inheritance of the Beloved.

Renewing the Mind: The Gateway to Freedom

Sustainable transformation doesn't begin in the body. It begins in the mind. Ephesians 4:22-23 calls us to a holy renovation, a reorientation of the entire self:

"You were taught, with regard to your former way of life, to put off your old self, which is being corrupted by its deceitful desires; to be made new in the attitude of your minds;" (NIV).

This is not behavior modification. This is identity reformation. The word Paul uses for "transformed" here is *metamorphoō* the same Greek word used to describe Jesus' transfiguration on the mountain. This isn't a surface-level change. It's a complete reordering of who we are, from the inside out. And it doesn't begin with what you do it begins with what you believe.

We have spent much of our lives chasing transformation through control: managing calories, perfecting routines, striving for approval, clinging to hustle. But true transformation the kind that endures, that brings peace, that frees us can't be forced. It must be *received*. It requires us to surrender the thought patterns that have formed the scaffolding of our false self and trade them for the truth of who God says we are.

God created our minds with the ability to adapt and grow. Our thoughts and actions can rewire the way we respond to life. Beliefs are not just abstract concepts they are embodied neural patterns. Every time we choose to think with the mind of Christ (1 Corinthians 2:16), we are rewiring pathways. We are forming new grooves in the brain that make peace more familiar than fear, rest more available than striving, and love more accessible than shame.

But we can't renew a mind we haven't made room for. Renewal requires repentance *metanoia* a turning away from the world's patterns of scarcity, self-reliance, and shame, and turning toward the truth that we are not our bodies, our past, or our performance. We are the Beloved. This truth doesn't erase our struggles, but it reframes them. It gives us permission to stop performing for transformation and start participating in it through presence, through practice, through grace.

I've seen this play out in the bodies and stories of women I've had the honor to serve from ministry leaders to mothers, from fitness enthusiasts to women incarcerated in prison facilities. No matter where they are or what they've done, one thing is true for all: behavior follows belief. And when the belief is anchored in God's truth not culture, not trauma, not comparison. The transformation that flows from it is not only possible; it's sustainable.

This is the invitation of *The Embodied Beloved*: to stop chasing worth through effort, and instead to become rooted in truth through renewal. We don't need to work harder to be holy. We need to receive the holiness already offered in Christ. And as our minds are renewed, our bodies will respond in kind. With movement marked by freedom, nourishment guided by wisdom, and habits formed not from striving, but from surrender.

The mind is not immovable. It is malleable, moldable, and by God's grace renewable. Transformation is possible, down to the cellular level. The field of neuroplasticity, illuminated by researchers like Norman Doidge (2007), shows us that the brain is not a fixed structure but a dynamic, living system capable of adapting and rewiring. But neuroplasticity is just the beginning.

Every thought we entertain, every emotion we dwell on, and every habit we repeat either strengthens or weakens specific neural pathways. This process known as *Hebbian learning* teaches us that "neurons that fire together, wire together." What we meditate on, we become. And when we meditate on God's Word, we become conformed to the mind of Christ.

This is more than a scientific observation. It's a deeply spiritual truth. Paul's charge in *Philippians 4:8* isn't poetic fluff; it's a neurological invitation.

> *"Finally, brothers and sisters, whatever is true, whatever is noble, whatever is right, whatever is pure, whatever is lovely, whatever is admirable if anything is excellent or praiseworthy think about such things."*

The Greek word for "mind" used in the New Testament *nous* doesn't just refer to intellect; it encompasses our beliefs, desires, imagination, and discernment. Renewal, then, isn't just downloading new information. It's experiencing a cognitive restructuring a Spirit-led reordering of how we interpret, filter, and respond to the world around us.

Every time we choose gratitude over grumbling, truth over toxic shame, or Scripture over spiraling thoughts, we are not just surviving. We are reshaping the architecture of our brains. We're laying down holy neural pathways. Pathways that allow our thoughts to travel toward peace instead of panic, toward hope instead of despair. This is the neurological map of transformation.

But let's be honest: this path is not always smooth. Trauma, chronic stress, and shame distort our internal compass. They rewire our bodies to expect danger rather than peace. The amygdala, our brain's built-in alarm system, becomes overactive. The prefrontal cortex, where faith, logic, and executive function reside, often goes offline. We stop responding from truth and start reacting from fear. And this disconnection doesn't stay in our heads. It shows up in our bodies: shallow breathing, clenched jaws, digestive distress, racing hearts, frozen postures.

Yet even here, especially here, there is hope. Because God didn't just create our minds to be renewed. He created our bodies to heal. Emerging fields like neurotheology reveal how spiritual practices like prayer, worship, and Scripture meditation reshape the brain, quiet the fear centers, and awaken compassion and clarity. Research on heart-brain coherence shows that when we cultivate states like gratitude, love, and awe. When we align our hearts and minds with God's truth. Our entire nervous system shifts from chaos to calm.

And from a biblical lens, this is the essence of *metanoia* the Greek word for repentance. Not just a change of behavior, but a change of mind and direction. A turning. A transformation. A returning to the truth of who God is, and who we are in Him.

This is why Spirit-led practices like breath prayer, somatic grounding, trauma-informed movement, and nervous system regulation aren't just wellness trends. They are tools of sanctification. They help us inhabit the truth we already know. With every slow breath surrendered to God, with every Scripture spoken into our bodies and bones, we are not just coping. We are being conformed.

Freedom, then, is not merely spiritual. It is physiological. To renew the mind is to rewire the nervous system. To meditate on God's Word is to give our bodies a new internal GPS: one marked by safety, sufficiency, and divine identity. It's one thing to *know* you are loved. It's another to *feel* it in your chest. To *breathe* it in. To *walk* it out.

This is the divine integration of spirit and science, of belief and biology. This is the path of the Embodied Beloved.

Selah Moment: Breath Prayer

Inhale: I am already free.
Exhale: I will live like it.

Use this breath prayer when old chains try to whisper that you are still captive.

Signs You Are Living a Mindset of Freedom
Freedom is not the absence of fear or the elimination of struggle. It is the unwavering awareness of who holds you in the storm, and the choice to live from that truth, not from your trauma. The embodied beloved walks in this freedom, not perfectly, but persistently.

You begin to notice when fear shows up. It still speaks, but its voice has lost authority. Our brains are shaped by what we repeatedly believe and rehearse. When fear used to sound like truth, you followed it out of habit. But now, you pause. You take a breath. You remember that the voice of fear is not the voice of your Father. And you don't obey it.

For the Spirit God gave us does not make us timid, but gives us power, love and self-discipline.
2 Timothy 1:7

You no longer chase perfectionism to earn your place. Instead, you root your choices in faith. A faith that believes you are being sanctified in process, not perfection. You understand that perfectionism is a form of self-preservation, a strategy the mind creates when it feels unsafe. But you've exchanged that fragile scaffolding for the firm foundation of grace.

Your worth is no longer attached to your outcomes, your productivity, or your performance. You are learning. Sometimes slowly, always beautifully. That your value was settled at the Cross. This allows you to rest, not resign. To work, not to prove. To show up fully, not to earn belonging but because you already belong.

You hear the voice of the Shepherd more clearly than the voice of shame; that's Rhema. In Scripture, *Rhema* refers to the spoken, living word of God. A word that is not just read but received, not just studied but *heard* in the spirit. It is the Word that meets you in the moment: timely, intimate, and personal.

His Rhema doesn't rush you. It doesn't crush you. It doesn't compare you to anyone else. It steadies you. It speaks peace into your chaos. It whispers truth when lies scream loud. It gently leads you beside still waters even as the world demands you hustle harder.

Shame may still try to echo in your nervous system through tension in your chest, clenched jaws, racing thoughts, but your soul is tuning itself to the frequency of love. And love has a sound. It sounds like stillness. Like grace. Like Jesus.

When the Rhema of God moves through you, it's not just information it's transformation. It realigns your spirit, renews your mind, and calms your body. You're not just hearing *any* voice. You're hearing the Good Shepherd, and His voice always leads to life.

When you fall, you recover faster. Not because you're stronger, but because you know you're already loved. Shame no longer gets to spiral you into self-punishment. Instead, you rise clothed in mercy, anchored in identity, reoriented by truth.

This is the mindset of freedom. Not ease, but embodiment. Not perfection, but presence. Not hustle, but holy abiding.

It's not the easy street. It's the narrow way. A daily choice to return to truth. To live attuned, not distracted. Anchored, not anxious. It takes intentional effort and Spirit-led surrender.

Because freedom isn't found in doing more, but in abiding more. It may not always feel easy, but it will lead you to peace real, rooted, peace that passes understanding.

Freedom is not the absence of struggle. Freedom is knowing whose you are, and choosing to live like it, even in the struggle.

How to Cultivate a Mindset of Freedom

1. Take Every Thought Captive
"We demolish arguments and every pretension that sets itself up against the knowledge of God, and we take captive every thought to make it obedient to Christ." (2 Corinthians 10:5, NIV)

Freedom starts by noticing what thoughts are running through your mind, and bringing them into the light. Name them. Examine them. Surrender them.

2. Practice Thought Replacement
When you catch a lie ("I'm failing. I'm behind. I'll never change."), replace it immediately with truth:
"I am a new creation." (2 Corinthians 5:17)
"I have everything I need for life and godliness." (2 Peter 1:3)

3. Meditate on Scripture Daily
Neuroscientists have found that focused meditation changes the brain's default pathways from anxiety and self-criticism toward peace and resilience (Luders et al., 2009).
Meditating on the living Word rewires us with divine truth.

4. Speak Freedom Over Your Body
Your body listens to your mind. Declare truth aloud:
"I am loved."
"My body is not a project. It's a temple."
"I move and nourish myself in freedom, not fear."

The Power of "I Am": Identity in Word and Wiring

Before freedom becomes a feeling or a choice, it begins with a name. And that name starts with "I am." These two words are more than a grammatical construction. They are a declaration of identity. A spiritual stake in the ground. And they hold power creative, generational, neurological power.

In Exodus 3:14, when Moses asks God for His name, God replies, *"I AM WHO I AM."* The Hebrew *Ehyeh Asher Ehyeh* can also be rendered as *"I will be what I will be."* In this divine utterance, God reveals not only His eternal self-existence but also His covenantal nearness: ever-present, ever-becoming, ever-enough.

When we speak "I am," we are echoing this divine pattern. Not as equals to God, but as image-bearers. What follows those two words often becomes the script we live by. "I am strong." "I am stupid." "I am enough." "I am a failure." Each declaration is more than psychological. It is physiological. Because the brain listens. And it builds.

Neuroscientifically, every "I am" statement activates the brain's reticular activating system (RAS) the gatekeeper of attention and focus. When you say "I am unlovable," your RAS begins to filter your experiences to affirm that belief. When you say "I am loved," your brain starts looking for evidence to confirm it. This is not wishful thinking. It's wiring.

Through Hebbian learning ("neurons that fire together wire together"), the more we repeat a phrase especially one about ourselves. The stronger and more automatic that thought becomes. Over time, these declarations carve grooves in the brain, shaping how we see, feel, act, and relate. Identity isn't just formed by experiences. It's forged by repetition.

This is why Scripture emphasizes the renewing of the mind and the power of the tongue. Proverbs 18:21 tells us, *"The tongue has the power of life and death."* James compares the tongue to a rudder. Small but capable of steering the entire ship. What you say shapes where you go.

Theologically, our identity must begin with what God says is true not what trauma, culture, or comparison has tried to name us. When Jesus says, *"I am the vine, you are the branches"* (John 15:5), He is not offering a motivational slogan. He is giving us an identity tethered to connection, nourishment, and growth. When we say, "I am the Beloved," we are not inventing something new. We are agreeing with Heaven.

So we must be careful with our "I am" statements. They are not just reflections. They are reinforcements. They build neurological highways and spiritual agreements. Every time we say, "I am tired, I am failing, I am not enough," we reinforce a script that the Enemy is all too eager to keep us rehearsing. But when we say, "I am chosen, I am being renewed, I am not what I've done. I am who He says I am," we are speaking freedom into our very cells.

And when that truth is spoken aloud, with breath, it doesn't just stay in the brain. It moves into the body. Our posture changes. Our breath slows. Our parasympathetic nervous system begins to activate. This is embodiment: truth spoken, truth heard, truth felt. Because God's words do not return void. And neither do ours.

So let the "I am" you speak match the "I AM" who made you. Speak from the Vine, not the void. And let every declaration shape you not into who the world says you should be, but into who God has already declared you are.

Reflection Prompts

1. What mental scripts have kept you in cycles of fear, striving, or perfectionism?

2. Where is God inviting you to live from freedom instead of fear?

3. How can you renew your mind today with truth instead of condemnation?

4. What would it feel like to walk in freedom not someday, but right now?

Embodied Prayer
Father,
Thank You that in Christ, I am already free.
Thank You that freedom is not something I earn. It is something I receive.
Renew my mind today. Break every lie that still clings to my heart.
Teach me to think, breathe, and live as one who is already loved.
I surrender the mindset of striving.
I embrace the mindset of sonship and daughterhood.
Let my thoughts reflect Your truth.
Let my actions overflow from Your grace.
I choose to walk in the freedom You purchased for me.
In Jesus' name, Amen.

Covered & Held Stillness Practice
Chains Fall in Stillness

Setup:
Find a quiet space. Sit or lie down, hands open on your lap or heart.

Practice:
As you breathe slowly, imagine every old chain (fear, shame, perfectionism) falling off you one by one.
Breathe in truth:
"I am free."
Breathe out lies:
"I am not captive to fear."

After several minutes of slow breathing, whisper:
"I live in freedom. I walk in light. I am the Beloved."

Movement-Based Practice
Freedom Walk

Setup:
Go for a gentle, intentional walk.

Practice:
With every step, imagine you are walking *out* of the old mindsets and *into* freedom.
With each step, repeat:
"I step into freedom."
"I step into grace."

Let your movement be a prophetic act of walking in what is already yours.

Chapter 7: The Gut–Heart–Brain Connection

The Beloved Speaks

"I always thought I was just overly sensitive or anxious. I would feel things deeply. My stomach churned with stress, my heart raced with fear, and my mind spiraled with anxious thoughts. I didn't understand then how intricately connected these sensations were, nor how deeply emotional wounds had embedded themselves into my physical being. But when Coach De began educating the connection between my gut, heart, and brain through God's design, my healing finally became tangible, embodied, and real."
-The Beloved

We are not fragmented beings. God designed us as intricately connected, embodied souls, every system, every cell, every feeling interwoven with divine intentionality.

For you created my inmost being; you knit me together in my mother's womb. I praise you because I am fearfully and wonderfully made;your works are wonderful,I know that full well. Psalm 139:13–14.

The gut, the heart, and the brain are not isolated control centers. They are a divine trinity within our body, three centers of intelligence, each playing a role in how we perceive, process, and carry the emotional weight of our lived experiences. In Hebrew understanding, the heart (lev) was never just a physical organ but the seat of thought, will, and emotion.

The gut, what the ancients would have called the bowels, was often referred to as the center of compassion and deep feeling (Philippians 2:1, KJV). And today, the truths of Scripture are being echoed in today's scientific discoveries: the gut has over 100 million neurons, communicates with the brain through the vagus nerve, and produces nearly 95% of the body's serotonin. This "second brain" is a living archive of emotional memory.

So many of us carry unprocessed emotions in our body like baggage we never agreed to hold. Trauma, stress, shame, and fear do not just live in our thoughts they live in our tissue, posture, digestion, breath, and nervous system. When Scripture says that *"a crushed spirit dries up the bones"* (Proverbs 17:22), it's not a metaphor. It's medicine. Science has shown that chronic stress and emotional suppression can weaken the immune system, disrupt gut function, dysregulate heart rhythms, and impair cognition. But the Lord has always known this. His Word told us that peace is life to the body (Proverbs 14:30), and now research tells us that joy, connection, and safety activate healing pathways in the brain and gut.

When we suppress emotions, especially painful ones, we don't eliminate them. We internalize them. We bury them in the gut. We guard our hearts. We numb the mind. But in the economy of God, healing is not avoidance it is integration. Wholeness is not about pretending we are okay. It's about allowing the Holy Spirit to meet us in our not-okayness and minister healing in every layer: body, soul, and spirit.

This is why the practice of embodiment is so refining. When we learn to listen to the language of the body. The clenched jaw, the tight shoulders, the churn in our gut. We begin to realize that our body is not betraying us. It's bearing witness. Emotions are not the enemy; they are messengers. The tears you choke down, the stomach pain that flares with anxiety, the fatigue that follows emotional suppression, these are all signals. God speaks through them. And when we ignore or override them, we silence a part of our story. He wants to heal.

But here's the good news: the same body that stores pain is the body God uses to release it. Through breath, movement, and presence, we activate the parasympathetic nervous system. The rest-and-digest or what I like to say, "rest-and-process" mode where the body feels safe enough to heal.

Deep diaphragmatic breathing, for example, sends signals through the vagus nerve to calm the heart and soothe the brain. It tells the gut: you are safe. This is not woo-woo. It is worshipful. It is a form of submission, of entrusting your body back into the hands of the Potter.

Jesus did not just come to redeem your soul. He came to restore your whole being. When He healed the hemorrhaging woman (Luke 8:43–48), He told her, *"Your faith has made you whole"* sozo, a Greek word that means to save, heal, and restore. That healing was not just spiritual. It was embodied. She felt it in her body the moment she touched His garment. And beloved, you too are invited into this kind of embodied wholeness not just the absence of pain, but the presence of peace.

To walk the path of wholeness is to walk with awareness. It's learning to ask,

What is my body saying that I haven't had the courage to hear?

It's learning to pause, breathe, and invite God into the very places you've tried to ignore your gut reactions, your heartaches, your mind loops. It's letting the Spirit bring coherence between your brain, heart, and gut until your whole self is aligned with truth.

You are not too much. You are not broken beyond repair. You are not a problem to be fixed but a beloved temple being rebuilt.

Let this chapter be your permission to feel again. To listen inward. To respond with compassion instead of condemnation. And to trust that the same God who raised Jesus from the dead is the same God who lives in you rewiring, renewing, and restoring your gut, your heart, and your mind into divine harmony.

You are the Embodied Beloved. And your wholeness begins not just with belief, but with embodiment.

A Divine Design for Wholeness

You are fearfully and wonderfully made not as isolated parts but as a beautifully interconnected whole. Scripture has always held the truth, science is only now beginning to echo it: your gut, your heart, and your brain form a remarkable triad of embodied wisdom, constantly communicating and shaping your emotional, physical, and spiritual experience.

God intentionally designed these three centers your gut, heart, and brain. To work harmoniously, helping you navigate life holistically. But trauma, stress, and emotional pain can disrupt this connection, leaving you disconnected, confused, and struggling in isolation.

Science Confirms What Scripture Reveals

Modern research confirms that your gut, heart, and brain communicate via the vagus nerve, a critical nerve running through your entire body, acting as a two-way communication highway.

Your gut is often called your "second brain" due to its extensive network of neurons (the enteric nervous system), directly affecting mood, anxiety, and intuition. It produces neurotransmitters like serotonin, significantly impacting emotional well-being.

Your heart does far more than pump blood; it sends powerful electromagnetic signals influencing your emotional and physical state. Scientific research from the HeartMath Institute shows your heart's rhythms directly influence your brain's ability to process information, regulate stress, and create feelings of calm or chaos.

Your brain, responsive to inputs from both your gut and heart, creates neural pathways shaped by your experiences, beliefs, and emotional responses.

Selah Moment: Breath Prayer

Use this space to pause and breathe truth into your body.
Inhale: "God, restore my inner harmony."
Exhale: "I embrace Your peace in every cell."

Emotional Embodiment: How Pain Becomes Physical

Your body will sometimes send and sometimes speak through discomfort. That persistent gut ache, the tension in your chest, the brain fog that won't lift, these may not be random. They may be the residue of pain your mind has tried to suppress and your soul hasn't yet processed. This is what I call *emotional embodiment*: the way unresolved heartache shows up in physical form.

God designed your body with extraordinary intelligence and integration. He knit you together so intricately that your emotional and physiological systems are constantly in dialogue. And when that dialogue is interrupted by trauma, by prolonged stress, by loss that was never grieved, your body doesn't forget. It remembers. It adapts. It holds what wasn't released.

No wonder when we experience chronic anxiety or unprocessed trauma, we often feel it in our digestive system. IBS, bloating, or other unexplained discomforts are frequently the body's cry for emotional regulation.

The heart, too, carries emotional memory. Cardiologists now recognize that stress-induced cardiomyopathy commonly called "broken heart syndrome" can mimic heart attacks in individuals experiencing extreme grief or trauma. Your heart actually responds to emotional weight.

The brain, intricately connected with your gut and heart through the nervous and endocrine systems, reflects emotional and physiological imbalance as anxiety, depression, cognitive fog, and burnout. Chronic emotional stress, whether stored in your gut as digestive disturbances, felt in your heart as persistent tension, or replayed in your mind as anxious loops often dysregulates the hypothalamic-pituitary-adrenal (HPA) axis. This critical pathway influences hormone production, inflammatory responses, and neurotransmitter balance.

Many women experiencing gut discomfort, heart palpitations, or chronic emotional overwhelm are diagnosed with "adrenal fatigue," especially when excessive exercise or prolonged stress contributes to their symptoms. Although commonly referred to as adrenal fatigue, the Endocrine Society clarifies that this condition is more accurately termed HPA axis dysfunction (Endocrine Society, 2016). This precise term emphasizes that healing requires addressing the root emotional and physiological connections between your gut, heart, and brain, rather than simply treating isolated symptoms.

But beloved, this connection isn't a flaw it's divine design. God created your body as an integrated whole. Not compartmentalized. Not fractured. Not a shell to carry your spirit, but a sacred vessel that mirrors the condition of your inner world. When your body cries out in pain, it may be alerting you to a deeper story beneath the surface: unforgiven grief, buried fear, shame dressed as performance. And those signals are not punishments. They are *invitations to healing*.

> *"The spirit of a man can endure his sickness, but a broken spirit who can bear?"* (Proverbs 18:14)

> *"A heart at peace gives life to the body"* (Proverbs 14:30).

This is theology meeting physiology: your healing begins when you stop silencing the body and start listening to it with compassion and curiosity.

In Scripture, we see embodied emotion everywhere. Jesus wept. He groaned. He sweated blood in Gethsemane. He didn't bypass His body to express pain. He allowed it to move through Him in surrender. And He invites us into the same: *a life of embodied presence, not disembodied performance.*

So if you're experiencing persistent symptoms in your gut, your heart, your mind, pause. Breathe.

Ask:

What truth have I not yet made space for?

What pain have I avoided naming?

What emotion is stuck in my flesh, waiting for permission to be released?

You are not fragile. You are fearfully and wonderfully made (Psalm 139:14). Your pain is not proof of failure, it is often the first sign that healing is on its way.

God doesn't bypass the body to reach the soul. He inhabits it. And in that sacred embodiment, healing begins.

Theological Integration: God's Design for Embodied Wholeness

Wholeness was always God's intention. From the beginning, He formed us not in fragments but in full integration spirit, soul, and body woven together in perfect harmony. We were not designed to live disembodied lives, separating faith from flesh or spirit from sensation. We were made to *embody* the love, presence, and peace of God in every cell, thought, emotion, and breath.

In the Hebrew worldview, the word for "heart" (*lev*) doesn't simply refer to emotion. It's the seat of your entire inner being, your thoughts, desires, emotions, will, and spiritual essence. The heart was not isolated from the body; it was the integrative center of the whole person. That's why Proverbs tells us:

> *"Above all else, guard your heart, for everything you do flows from it."*
> — Proverbs 4:23 (NIV)

Everything. Your habits. Your words. Your posture. Your appetite. Your emotional reactions. All of it is downstream from the state of your heart. Paul echoes this beautifully in his letter to the Philippians:

> *"And the peace of God, which transcends all understanding, will guard your hearts and your minds in Christ Jesus."*
> — Philippians 4:7 (NIV)

Notice that peace is not just an idea, it's embodied protection. It stands guard over your *heart* (emotional core) and your *mind* (cognitive processing). This is not a metaphor, it's medicine. God's peace literally becomes a nervous system intervention, a spiritual recalibration, a physiological shift into safety and presence.

And long before you even had language to articulate emotion, your body was already telling a story of divine design. (Psalm 139:13–14) That "inmost being" is more than physical organs. It includes your soul, your gut, your spirit, your *nephesh* and your *ruach*. God didn't just create your body; He *knit* it intimately, intentionally, intricately. Every nerve, every hormone, every heartbeat was woven with care. And He declared it *good*.

So when you feel overwhelmed, dysregulated, or scattered, it doesn't mean you're broken; it means your design is working. Your body is alerting you to disconnection. It's not betraying you. It's beckoning you back to integration. That's not dysfunctional. That's divine feedback.

God's design for your healing is not compartmentalized. It's not only cognitive. It's not only spiritual. It's *embodied.* That means your healing won't just be something you *believe,* it will be something you *feel*, *live*, and *become*. It means peace won't just be a thought you try to hold onto, it will be a presence you begin to dwell in.

Wholeness is not an achievement, it's your inheritance in Christ. And as you return to God's design, you don't just reclaim your mind or your body, you reclaim your identity as the Beloved, fully known and fully integrated.

Reflection Prompts
1. How does emotional stress or trauma physically manifest in your gut, heart, or brain?
2. What have your gut feelings or heart sensations been trying to tell you?
3. How can understanding your embodied emotions change how you respond to stress?

Embodied Prayer
Father God,
I invite Your presence into my gut, heart, and mind. Unravel the emotional pain trapped within me. Reconnect and restore the pathways you've lovingly created. Let Your peace fill every fiber of my being. In Jesus name, Amen.

Covered & Held Stillness Practice
Guided Embodied Visualization:

1. Lie comfortably, hands resting on your belly and heart.
2. Visualize a warm, healing light representing God's presence flowing gently through your gut, calming every tense or anxious sensation.
3. Allow this light to expand upward to your heart, soothing emotional wounds and bringing peace.
4. Let it continue rising into your brain, calming racing thoughts, quieting mental chaos, and restoring clarity.
5. Stay in this peaceful embodied state for 5–10 minutes, sensing the harmonious connection God intends.

Movement Practice: Restoring Embodied Connection

1. Gentle Twist – Slowly twist side-to-side from the waist, releasing gut tension.
2. Heart-Opening Stretch– Open arms wide, gently arching your back to expand your chest, releasing emotional tightness.
3. Gentle Neck and Head Movements – Slowly move your head side to side and up and down, calming brain activity and tension.
4. Integrative Breathing– Deeply breathe, inhaling into the belly, then heart, then brain. Exhale fully, visualizing release of emotional tension.

Finish by returning to stillness, hands on heart and belly, quietly repeating:

> "I am whole, connected, and embodied through Christ's love."

Ready to put what you've read into practice?
Download the FaithFueled Life App and take your journey deeper. Inside, you'll find guided breath prayers, embodied movement sessions, Scripture meditations, and soul-strengthening practices that bring this book to life. Whether you're seeking stillness, strength, or spiritual renewal, the app gives you real-time tools to embody your faith and steward your temple; anytime, anywhere.

Don't just read about transformation. Live it. www.tinyurl.com/FAITHFUELEDAPP and begin your journey of becoming the Embodied Beloved.

Part 3: Reclaiming Movement

Embodied Worship

Your body is not a project to fix. It is a vessel to honor.
In this section, you'll learn to move, and live from a place of worship rather than warfare.

Movement becomes prayer.
Nourishment becomes praise.

You'll release punishment patterns and enter into rhythms of grace where strength, healing, and joy abide.

Chapter 8: Reclaiming Movement as a Spiritual Act

"For in him we live and move and have our being.' As some of your own poets have said, 'We are his offspring."
-Acts 17:28

The Beloved Speaks

"I used to work out to punish myself. To shrink. To 'make up' for food. It felt like penance. Then I heard Coach De say, 'Your workout can be worship.' That phrase wrecked me in the best way. I started walking with Jesus, not just toward a goal. I stretched with music that spoke to my spirit. I danced without needing to be smaller. Movement became sacred. It became prayer. And now, I don't move to fix my body. I move to honor it."
— The Beloved

What if your workout was worship?

What if your stretch was surrendered?

What if your sweat was sacred?

What if your whole body could become a living, breathing doxology?

For so many women, movement has been shaped by pressure, not praise.

We've been taught to burn calories, to shrink ourselves, to earn rest like a reward after punishment. We've been told that our worth increases when our waistlines decrease.

But the heartbeat of God invites us into a different story:

Movement was never meant to be punishment.

It was meant to be praise.

Have you ever heard the word doxology?

It's a rich, ancient word.

Doxology means "a declaration of glory," doxa meaning "glory" and logos meaning "word" or "speech." A doxology is a movement of the soul expressed in word, song, or body that magnifies God's beauty. It's when all of who we are, heart, mind, soul, and strength, reflect the One who made us.

We were designed to move in Him, through Him, and for Him. Not to earn love, but because we are already fully loved.

Romans 12:1 captures this beautifully:

"Therefore, I urge you, brothers and sisters, in view of God's mercy, to offer your bodies as a living sacrifice, holy and pleasing to God this is your true and proper worship." (NIV)

This Scripture is what convicted me on my own journey to move, eat, and live as an act of worship. It's what ignited a passionate conviction to not only live it but also share it with others.

When Paul says "bodies," he doesn't mean just our souls. He means our whole physical selves, our muscles, our breath, our sweat, our stretch offered back to the Giver of Life as an act of worship. Movement becomes a living doxology when it shifts from striving to surrender. From earning to expressing. From pressure to presence.

For the Beloved Who Hates to Move:
Maybe movement feels like betrayal to you. Maybe your body aches, or fatigue has wrapped itself around your days like a heavy fog. Maybe you've only known movement through the lens of shame, comparison, and defeat. I understand more than you know.

For me, movement wasn't always a joy. It wasn't an expression of freedom. It was a punishment. I can still remember the sting of the summer sun on my skin as I was forced to run laps around our yard, tears blurring my vision, my legs trembling from exhaustion. Every mistake, every disobedience, was met with squats, push-ups, and sprints not as training, but as correction. My parents didn't use corporal punishment to discipline us. They used physical exercise. Planks or wall sit until you collapse for our disobedient actions. My body was treated like a problem to be disciplined, not a temple to be treasured.

Movement became a symbol of failure, not celebration. Sweat became a scarlet letter of shame, not holy surrender. Even long after the punishments stopped, my nervous system still remembered.

My body carried the story, even when I tried to move past it. Maybe your body remembers, too. Maybe you carry a story of movement shaped more by fear than by freedom.

But hear me, Beloved:

God is not standing over you with a whistle and a clipboard. He's not keeping score or tallying your failures. He's not waiting for you to collapse in exhaustion to deem you worthy.

He invites you, tenderly, patiently, to come alive again. Not through pressure, but through presence. Not through punishment, but through praise. Movement, even the smallest stretch, can be a sacred act of being with Him.

A gentle walk. A deep breath. A sway to a song that lifts your heart. Every small movement can become a wordless prayer: "Here I am, Lord. I'm still yours."

Gentle movement like stretching, walking, or slow strength work has been shown to regulate the nervous system, calm the amygdala (the brain's fear center), and increase serotonin (the "peace" chemical) (Ratey, 2008).

In simple terms, moving your body actually helps you feel safe again. It pulls you out of the swirl of anxiety and plants you back into the present moment, back into the sacred now, where God meets you. It can be redeemed even if it was misused You don't have to move hard to move holy. You simply have to move with Him.

Selah Moment: Breath Prayer

Inhale: This movement is worship.
Exhale: This body is Your temple.

Repeat as you walk, stretch, or sit in stillness.

For the Beloved Who Has Obsessed Over Movement:

Maybe movement has been a different kind of chain for you. Maybe you've lived in the land of extremes, pushing, striving, punishing your body under the banner of "health" or "discipline."

Exercise was once your altar and your body, the sacrifice. You've believed the lie that if you just work harder, sweat more, shrink further, you'll finally be enough.

But beloved, hear me:

Your body is not a project to fix. It's already a miracle to honor. You don't move to earn God's love. You move because you are already His beloved daughter.

Jesus says:

"Come to me, all you who are weary and burdened, and I will give you rest." (Matthew 11:28, NIV)

Even your movement can be rest when it's rooted in love. You were made to move from fullness, not from lack. You were made to praise with your body, not punish it.

And science affirms the harm of obsession too:

Chronic over-exercise can elevate cortisol (the stress hormone) and impair metabolic health, leading to inflammation, hormone disruption, and even emotional instability (Hackney, 2006). In other words, living on the treadmill of "not enough" doesn't make you healthier. It slowly depletes you.

God's rhythms are kinder. His yoke is easy. His burden is light (Matthew 11:30).

And His invitation stands: Move with Me, not apart from Me.

The Power of Praise in Movement

When we move as an act of praise, everything shifts. Praise rewires your mind: Studies show that gratitude and worship reshape neural pathways, reducing anxiety and increasing resilience (Fox et al., 2015). Moving while worshiping literally retrains your brain to hope again.

Praise restores your body: Gentle rhythmic movement (like walking, dancing, stretching) calms the sympathetic nervous system (the "fight or flight" response) and strengthens the parasympathetic (the "rest and digest" state), helping your body heal.

Praise renews your spirit: Scripture reminds us that God inhabits the praises of His people (Psalm 22:3). When you move in praise, you create a dwelling place for Him right there in the stretch, in the sweat, in the breath.

Movement becomes a holy echo. The body joins the spirit to say,

"Glory to God from whom all blessings flow."

So what if today, you moved differently?

What if you didn't stretch to punish, but to praise?

What if you didn't sweat to strive, but to surrender?

What if every breath, every step, every heartbeat became a whispered doxology?

You don't have to move perfectly.

You just have to move in love.

He's not asking for performance.

He's inviting you into praise.

From Performance to Presence

For too long, we've lived under the illusion that our spiritual life is something that happens in our heads or hearts, while our bodies are either ignored, punished, or pushed beyond their limits in pursuit of perfection. But from Genesis to Revelation, God never separates the body from the spirit. The way we move, eat, breathe, rest, and labor is all part of the divine rhythm of worship. You were never meant to perform holiness with your mind and neglect your body in the process. You were meant to *embody it*.

In the ancient Hebrew imagination, worship was never still. It was physical. Movement and posture were forms of praise. The Psalms are full of instructions to bow low, raise hands, kneel, dance, clap, lie prostrate, and shout aloud. These weren't symbolic gestures.

They were embodied expressions of reverence, surrender, and joy. When David danced before the Lord with all his might (2 Samuel 6:14), he wasn't performing for an audience. He was fully present with the One who made him. His body was not an obstacle to holiness, it was an instrument of worship.

Jesus, too, embodied presence. He walked miles from village to village. He knelt in the dirt to restore dignity. He broke bread, washed feet, and bled from His body to reconcile ours. Every step He took was a sermon. Every movement, a revelation of love made flesh. Even after His resurrection, His glorified body bore the scars of redemption as evidence of embodied sacrifice.

And the early church followed in His footsteps literally. They didn't sit in pews or scroll screens. They moved from house to house, breaking bread in real communities, worshiping not just with their voices but with their whole lives. Their spirituality wasn't theoretical, it was incarnational.

> *"Do you not know that your bodies are temples of the Holy Spirit, who is in you, whom you have received from God?... Therefore honor God with your bodies."* — 1 Corinthians 6:19–20 (NIV)

This isn't a guilt trip. It's an invitation. God doesn't want your performance. He wants your presence. And presence requires embodiment.

Your body is not a problem to fix. It's a vessel to offer. A temple that holds the indwelling Spirit. And one of the most powerful offerings you can bring is movement not to burn calories or earn approval, but to return to the God who made your limbs, lungs, and life for worship. Could you show up to your workouts different if it wasnt out of obligation but was a commitment?

Whether you're walking in silence, stretching in surrender, dancing in joy, or simply breathing with intention, your body becomes a sanctuary. Not for shame. Not for striving. But for sacred presence. Let go of performance. Return to presence. Your wholeness begins here.

How We Lost Sacred Movement
Somewhere along the way, the movement lost its sacredness. It was never meant to be a punishment. Never meant to be a way to shrink, erase, or correct the bodies God declared good. And yet, for many of us especially as Christian women, the relationship between faith, fitness, and the body has been distorted.

Instead of holy embodiment, we've inherited hustle, comparison, and shame. Movement became a means to control rather than connect. Rest became a luxury, not a birthright. Our bodies were no longer seen as sacred space but as spiritual distractions or vanity projects.

We internalized this narrative: that smaller meant better, stillness meant laziness, and only the soul mattered to God. In that disconnection, we lost something vital.

Some of us swung into the deep end of secular fitness culture, obsessing over metrics, chasing the perfect physique, and measuring our worth by external transformation. We baptized body obsession in Christian language, but the striving remained rooted in fear. Others detached completely, convinced that the body was too fleshly to be holy, too burdensome to be a blessing. Movement became optional at best and sinful at worst. In both extremes, we lost sight of what God designed from the very beginning of integration.

But Scripture calls us back not to performance, but to presence. Not to punish, but to participate in divine design.

> "With what shall I come before the Lord and bow down before the exalted God? Shall I come before him with burnt offerings, with calves a year old? Will the Lord be pleased with thousands of rams, with ten thousand rivers of olive oil? Shall I offer my firstborn for my transgression,the fruit of my body for the sin of my soul? He has shown you, O mortal, what is good. And what does the Lord require of you? To act justly and to love mercy and to walk humbly with your God."
> — Micah 6:6–8 (NIV)

Do you see it? Walk humbly. Some versions say prudently meaning, in a way that shows care and thought for the future. There it is a movement of worship. Not flashy. Not pressured. But integrated. Embodied. A rhythm of justice, mercy, and humility lived out not just in your beliefs but in your body. The Hebrew word for "walk" (halak) implies ongoing motion in everyday life, step by step, journeying in pace with God.

From the beginning, you were created as an embodied soul, breath and dust, spirit and skin, fully fused by the hands of a loving Creator. To move is not to indulge the flesh. It is to inhabit the temple that God entrusted to you. Your stretch, your sweat, your stillness are not meaningless. They are invitations. Ways to practice presence. Ways to remember you're alive, loved, and held. In everything we do we are called to bring glory to God. Why would how we move be excluded?

You don't have to punish your body into submission to be faithful.
You don't have to ignore your body to be holy.
You were never meant to choose between your spirit and your skin.

In Christ, your body is not a battleground. It's a living testimony. Not a flaw to fix, it's a vessel of worship. Not a project, it's a place where God dwells.

Let this truth unclench your jaw.
Let it soften your breath.
Let it remind you: you're allowed to move in joy, not in shame.

You don't have to earn the right to rest.
You don't have to strive to be sacred.
You already are.

Reclaiming Holy Movement

To reclaim movement as a spiritual act is to move in order to connect, not to control. It is to listen to your body with kindness, not punish it with striving. It is to honor your season, your energy, and your story without comparison or shame.

Movement becomes more than motion. It becomes a conversation with God. A walk becomes a prayer, each step a quiet "Amen." A stretch becomes a surrender, a silent yielding to His love. A strength session becomes an altar, where effort and offering meet. A dance becomes delightful, the body rejoicing in the goodness of life.

You begin to feel His presence in your breath. You begin to hear His whisper in your heartbeat. You begin to praise Him with every step, every reach, every rhythm. You inhabit your body not to impress, not to perform, but to embody to bear witness to the truth:

You are His.

You are loved.

You are free.

I did my first Murph this Memorial Day, and it was a challenge. For those who don't know, the Murph is a hero workout done in honor of Navy Lieutenant Michael Murphy, who gave his life in service to our country. The workout includes a 1-mile run, 100 pullups, 200 pushups, 300 squats, and another 1-mile run all while wearing a weighted vest, if you choose. I did not choose to wear a vest.

Leading up to it, I had doubts about whether I was physically capable of doing it. But everything shifted when my heart posture changed.

I meditated on Scripture with every push up. I thanked the Lord with every pullup. I squatted to the rhythm of worship music. And when I ran; I praised.

What began as a physical challenge turned into a full-on hour of praise and worship. People even caught me dancing in between sets to my worship playlist! While others were exhausted tackling the workout alone, I was filled with joy, because I didn't do it alone. I invited the Lord into it, and He met me there. And that made all the difference. I was sore the next day but during the process it was an experience to praise and honor.

Freedom in Movement

Freedom doesn't mean you never follow a plan. It means your plan doesn't own you. You move because you *get to*, not because you *have to*. You train your body not for punishment but for *purpose*.

> *"I discipline my body like an athlete, training it to do what it should."* — 1 Corinthians 9:27 (NLT)

That's not control. That's stewardship.

What Science Says About Movement and Worship

Movement is one of God's tender gifts for regulating our bodies and restoring our hearts. Somatic research confirms what Scripture has long invited us to experience: when we move intentionally, cortisol, the stress hormone, begins to fall. Anxiety loosens its grip. Trauma stored deep in the body begins to untangle and release (van der Kolk, 2014). Movement becomes a way we physically participate in our own healing.

As we move, joy rises. Sustained, purposeful movement stirs the release of dopamine, serotonin, and endorphins. The very chemicals that lift our mood, clear our minds, and rebuild our sense of hope and self-worth (Ratey, 2008). It's not just a workout; it's a restoration of the spirit.

Mindful, embodied movement does even more. It awakens the prefrontal cortex, the part of the brain that helps us regulate emotions and create a sense of internal safety (Porges, 2011). Each breath, each step, each stretch becomes a way to rewire our brains for resilience, for calm, for connection.

When you move with Jesus, you're not just working out. You are restoring the sacred temple where He lovingly dwells. You are reclaiming the joy that fear tried to steal. You are releasing burdens you were never meant to carry. Movement isn't about fixing yourself. It's about finding yourself whole, beloved, and free in His presence.

Reflection Prompts

1. What messages have you received about movement, fitness, or your body that need healing?

2. How do you feel when you move, free, fearful, ashamed, joyful?

3. What kind of movement feels like *worship* to you?

4. How can you invite God into your movement this week?

Embodied Prayer

Father,
I surrender the way I've used movement to prove, punish, or perform.
Thank You for giving me a body that can move.
Help me honor it. Not in fear, but in freedom.
Teach me to move in worship. To stretch, walk, dance, and breathe with Your Spirit.

Let my movement reflect my love for You.
This body is Yours. This breath is Yours.
Let my temple move in step with You.
In Jesus' name, Amen.

Covered & Held Stillness Practice
Setup:

Lie on your back, feet flat or extended.
Place one hand over your heart and the other over your hip or ribcage.

Practice:
Breathe slowly and say aloud or silently:

> *"This is my temple. I do not need to earn rest."*

Feel your breath rise and fall under your hands.
Invite the Holy Spirit to inhabit your body, every joint, every cell.

Ask: *"Where have I moved to be seen by the world instead of being seen by You?"*

Let His presence settle into your body like peace.

Close with:

> *"I am covered. I am held. I am home in this temple."*

Movement-Based Exercise
Setup:
Choose a quiet space and a worship playlist that ministers to your spirit.

1. **Reach up** — Stretch tall as you inhale.
   Say: *"I offer this movement to You."*

2. **Fold forward or bow** — Exhale and soften.
   Say: *"I surrender my striving."*

3. **Lunge or side-stretch gently** — Hold for a few breaths.
   Say: *"Make me flexible in Your hands."*

4. **Finish kneeling or in child's pose** — Breathe deeply.
   Say: *"I don't have to move to be loved. I move because I am."*

This is your altar. Your rhythm. Your worship.

Ready to put what you've read into practice?
Download the FaithFueled Life App and take your journey deeper. Inside, you'll find guided breath prayers, embodied movement sessions, Scripture meditations, and soul-strengthening practices that bring this book to life. Whether you're seeking stillness, strength, or spiritual renewal, the app gives you real-time tools to embody your faith and steward your temple; anytime, anywhere.

Don't just read about transformation. Live it.
www.tinyurl.com/FAITHFUELEDAPP and begin your journey of becoming the Embodied Beloved.

Chapter 9: Sustainable Fitness for Your Season

*"There is a time for everything,
and a season for every activity under the heavens:"*-
Ecclesiastes 3:1

The Beloved Speaks

"I thought I had to go hard all the time. No excuses. No breaks. But it was breaking me. Every time life shifted kids, grief, work. I'd fall off track and spiral. It wasn't until Coach De encouraged me to embrace seasons that everything changed. Some weeks I walk. Some weeks I lift. Some weeks I just rest. I'm still consistent, but now it's flexible and full of grace. I stopped trying to 'bounce back' or 'get back on track ' Now I just keep showing up because that's what my season needs."
— The Beloved

You don't need another fitness plan. You need a rhythm that fits your real life. And I say that as someone who loves a good plan (I've even built an app full of them). But this isn't about chasing your "goal weight" life or waiting for the elusive "once I get it together" moment.

It's about honoring your right now. The life God has given you, the grace He's poured over you, and the body you're living in today. Sustainable fitness isn't rooted in intensity; it's rooted in integrity. It means showing up, not perfectly, but faithfully in the body you have, in the season you're in, with the energy and capacity you've been given. This is the kind of movement that transforms not just your body, but your whole life. This Chapter comes from lived out experience and something I've struggled with for many years but when I found freedom in rhythms it allowed me to show up differently.

Seasons Change And So Should Your Fitness

> *"There is a time for everything, and a season for every activity under the heavens."* —
> Ecclesiastes 3:1 (NIV)

You don't need another trendy fitness plan. You're far enough in this book to realize its much deeper. I want to offer you something sustaining. A rhythm that fits your real life. That takes you off of the guilt ride and allows you to live life. Don't misunderstand me. Movement and nourishing well is still essential but with grace over guilt it comes from a place of commitment and not an obligation. And I am saying that as someone who loves a good plan (I've even built an app filled with them). They're not trendy, they're functional. I also believe a strategic plan will help you get to where you want to be.

But there's a difference between rigid routines and holy rhythms. This isn't about chasing your "goal weight" or waiting for your "once I get it together" life to begin. It's about embracing your *right now God-given*, grace-filled life you're living today. Sustainable fitness isn't built on intensity; it's built on *integrity*. It's the quiet discipline of showing up imperfectly, but consistently in the body you have, in the season you're in, with the capacity you've been entrusted with. This kind of rhythm doesn't just shape your body; it transforms your relationship with movement, with yourself, and with the One who created you. This change keeps you consistent so that you no longer have to start up again.

Scripture reminds us, *"There is a time for everything, and a season for every activity under the heavens"* (Ecclesiastes 3:1).

For most of human history, movement was life. We didn't need memberships or motivation to move. Our bodies were naturally engaged through walking, harvesting, carrying, building, and simply living. From dawn to dusk, physical activity was integrated into our survival, our worship, and our way of being. But as society shifted from agrarian life to industrial work, and eventually to a digital economy, movement became optional.

Desks replaced fields. Screens replaced physical labor. And the rise of convenience created a world where our bodies could sit still all day and still function in the world. That's when we began to see movement not as a rhythm, but as a task to add an hour at the gym, a class in our schedule, a box to check. We stopped embodying our days, and started outsourcing our movement.

But God designed your life in seasons, and each one has its own tempo. Your movement should honor that. Some seasons are for strength and building. Others invite you to stretch, slow down, and recover. Some call you to rest and simply stay present. Science backs this sacred rhythm: studies show that exercise aligned with your nervous system's state; whether it's high-energy (sympathetic) or restorative (parasympathetic) can optimize mental health, hormone regulation, and longevity (Porges, 2011; Ratey, 2008). When we ignore the natural ebb and flow of our bodies and lives, we often burn out, get injured, or give up. But when we move with our bodies not against them we foster resilience, balance, and peace.

Sustainability doesn't come from what burns the most calories. It comes from what keeps you connected to your body, mind, and spirit over the long haul. Neuroscience calls this *interoceptive awareness*: the ability to sense and respond to what's going on inside your body (Craig, 2002). When cultivated through mindful movement, this awareness enhances emotional regulation, reduces stress, and increases self-compassion. In other words, movement becomes more than exercise. It becomes a spiritual practice. A way to tune into God's presence. A way to embody grace. You weren't created to hustle endlessly. You were made to walk with God in step, in sync, and in surrender. Let your fitness reflect that sacred invitation.

Grace for Every Season
There are so many seasons a woman walks through in her lifetime each one uniquely marked with joy and ache, surrender and strength. No two stories are exactly alike, yet there are threads that connect us: transitions, tensions, and the ever-present invitation to meet God right where we are.

Motherhood: Whether you're in the sleep-deprived haze of newborn days, managing the beautiful unpredictability of toddlers, navigating school schedules, or learning to release your grown children with open hands and a tender heart. Your energy shifts. Your time is no longer your own, and your body may feel like it belongs to everyone else but you.

And yet; God sees.

He is El Roi, the God who sees you (Genesis 16:13). He saw Hagar in the wilderness alone, exhausted, misunderstood, and He called her by name. He sees you, too. In this season, movement may look like rocking your baby as a sacred sway. A walk around the block may become your breathing space. Some days, stretching while folding laundry may be your only workout, and that is still worship when it's done with a heart turned toward Him.

Grief or Healing: When your heart is heavy or your body is recovering, the pace slows. The ache of loss, whether of a loved one, your health, a dream, or a former version of yourself demands tenderness.

You keep track of all my sorrows. You have collected all my tears in your bottle. You have recorded each one in your book. Psalm 56:8

And I want you to know if you're in these seasons or coming out please remember.

The Lord is close to the brokenhearted; he rescues those whose spirits are crushed. Psalm 34:18

You have to lean in because in this season, movement may be slow and sacred. A restorative stretch, a breath prayer in child's pose, or a walk with tears in your eyes. All of it can be holy ground. Healing is not linear, and God does not rush your process. He gently leads those with young (Isaiah 40:11), and He gently carries you, too.

Career Shifts or Ministry Growth: When God opens doors, assignments expand, or you're building something new, time becomes tight. Stewarding a calling doesn't always leave hours for elaborate workouts. But God doesn't need quantity to work with He blesses obedience.

A Scripture I often meditate and remind myself is,

"Whatever you do, work at it with all your heart, as working for the Lord." (Colossians 3:23).

In a season, a 15-minute strength session can be an altar. A walk between meetings can be a reset. It's not about how long. It's about where your heart is postured. Movement becomes a tool to sustain your assignment, not a distraction from it.

Mental Health Valleys: When the fog of anxiety or depression settles in, even the smallest acts feel enormous. Brushing your teeth can feel like a mountain. Lacing your shoes may require supernatural strength.

This is not failure.

This is the fight.

"Though I walk through the valley of the shadow of death, I will fear no evil, for You are with me." (Psalm 23:4)

In these seasons, showing up is the victory. Lifting your arms in worship even if they're trembling it is warfare. Choosing one minute of movement is a declaration: I'm still here, and God is still with me. We move because we are able. Remember through it all. You are not alone in your valley. He walks with you.

Busy, Joy-Filled Seasons: There are also seasons of celebration weddings, reunions, births, breakthroughs where your heart is full and your calendar is overflowing. In these moments, movement becomes delight.

"You turned my mourning into dancing; you removed my sackcloth and clothed me with joy." (Psalm 30:11).

Dance in the kitchen. Walk with a friend. Praise Him with every step. Let your body become a living hallelujah. In this season, exercise can be an extension of your joy. A way to praise the Giver of every good and perfect gift (James 1:17).

So in each and every season, pause and ask:

"What honors my temple right now?" (1 Corinthians 6:19–20)

Not, "What did I do last season?"

Not, "What is she doing?" Don't get distracted looking Sideways.

"Keep your eyes fixed on the things above. Not the things of this world." Colossians 3:2

But what honors this body, this soul, this moment with God?

Because honoring your temple is not about perfection or performance. It's about presence. It's about listening.

It's about trusting that your body is not just a project. It's a place where the Holy Spirit dwells. And in every season, He is faithful to meet you there.

In each season, ask:

"What honors my temple right now?"

Selah Moment: Breath Prayer

Inhale: I move with grace.
Exhale: I honor this season.

Breathe that in as a daily reminder.

Building a Sustainable Fitness Rhythm

This is not about chasing perfection. It's about choosing a pattern. A holy rhythm that honors your body, your story, and your season. It's not about punishing your body into submission. It's about partnering with it, with kindness and trust, and inviting God into the process.

I don't want you to walk away from this book clutching a rigid 30-day challenge or another list of rules you'll feel guilty for not following.

I want you to walk away equipped anchored in truth for the moments when you feel tempted by the quick fix, the cleanse, the "lose 10 lbs in 10 days" hype.

Here's how to realign your movement with your faith and your season:

1. Start with your why.
Before you lace up your shoes or hit play on a workout, pause and ask:

Why am I doing this?

Is it to lose weight or to steward the temple God gave you?
Is it to shape your image or to walk in integrity and wholeness?

One leads to striving. The other leads to peace.
Movement done from love, not for approval, is the kind that lasts.

"Whatever you do, do it all for the glory of God." (1 Corinthians 10:31)

2. Choose joyful movement.
The world may tell you that exercise needs to feel like punishment to count.

But joy is a fruit of the Spirit (Galatians 5:22), not guilt.
God made your body to move, and He delights in your delight. You are allowed to smile during your workout. You are allowed to dance, walk, stretch, lift, or sway, and count it as worship. If it brings you life and helps you show up more fully, it's enough.

3. Be flexible with your structure.
Discipline is good, but rigidity isn't the goal.
Set intentions, not ultimatums.
Maybe you aim for three workouts this week, and life hands you two. That's not failure. That's wisdom to adjust.
Jesus Himself withdrew often to rest and pray (Luke 5:16).

You have permission to shift your schedule without shame.
You're not weak you're responding with grace.

4. Match movement to your energy.
Your energy is not a moral issue.

Some days, you'll feel a strong movement with power.
Some days, you'll feel tender move with gentleness.
Some days, you'll feel weary and don't move at all.
That, too, is holy.

Let your movement be an act of listening. Let your body's needs inform your choices.
This is how we walk in step with the Spirit by honoring the temple, not overriding it.

5. Remember: small is sacred.
Ten minutes of grace-filled movement is more powerful than an hour of guilt-fueled striving or no movement at all.

The world will try to convince you that "more" is always better. But Jesus praised the widow's mite. The small gift given in faith (Mark 12:41–44).

Your five-minute walk with Jesus? It matters.
Your stretch session after bedtime stories? It's enough.
Your breathwork between meetings? Sacred.
You don't need a perfect plan. You need a posture of grace.

A rhythm rooted in love, not lack.
And a deep belief that honoring your temple is not a task to complete, but a life to live. One breath, one step, one surrendered movement at a time.

Signs Your Fitness Is Sustainable

How do you know if your fitness rhythm is truly serving your soul, not just your schedule?

Look for these fruits. Sustainable fitness isn't just measured in reps or results. It's revealed in the way it shapes your spirit. You feel refreshed instead of depleted. After movement, you don't feel emptied. You feel renewed. It may be hard, yes. Sweat may fall. But you walk away with more peace, more breath, more presence.

"Come to me, ALL YOU who are weary and burdened, and I will give you rest.." (Matthew 11:28)

Sustainable movement gives life, it doesn't drain it. You move because you want to, not because you have to. Your motivation flows from freedom, not fear. It's not driven by guilt, comparison, or diet culture pressure. You move because you get to steward this temple not because you're trying to earn worth.

"It is for freedom that Christ has set us free. Stand firm, then, and do not let yourselves be burdened again by a yoke of slavery." (Galatians 5:1)

You can adapt without shame. If the day goes sideways and your planned workout becomes a walk or rest you don't spiral into condemnation. You adjust with grace because you're living from a relationship, not a rigid rulebook. His mercies are new every morning. (Lamentations 3:22–23) So is your fitness rhythm.

You speak kindly to yourself when you miss a workout. Your inner voice mirrors the gentleness of Christ, not the harshness of culture. You don't shame yourself. You shepherd yourself.

"You didn't fail. You listened. You'll try again tomorrow."

This is the fruit of self-control and gentleness, not self-criticism. (Galatians 5:22–23)

You see movement as part of worship, not punishment.
Fitness becomes a space to encounter God, not earn His approval.
You stretch like you're surrendering.
You lift like you're training for purpose.
You walk like you're praying with each step.

"This is my living sacrifice and act of worship" (Romans 12:1)

And it's beautiful to Him.

What Science Says About Sustainable Fitness

God's Word proves true again and again not because He needs to prove Himself, but because truth can't help but reveal itself. Scripture has always declared what science is only beginning to understand: that our bodies were not created for punishment, but for partnership. We are not machines to be managed. We are temples to be tended.

Modern research confirms what the Spirit has been whispering all along:

Rigid and perfection-driven exercise plans often lead to burnout, overtraining, and injury. The body breaks down when we push it without mercy. But when we approach movement with joy and flexibility. When we release the pressure to perform. We begin to flourish. (Cavill et al., 2006)

Grace-filled fitness, rooted in self-compassion, leads to greater consistency and self-worth. When we stop shaming ourselves into discipline and instead train with kindness, our motivation becomes sustainable. This isn't weakness, it's wisdom. (Semenchuk et al., 2018)

Rhythmic, intentional movement like walking, dancing, or flowing with the breath. Does more than strengthen the body. It heals. It restores. It regulates emotion and anchors us in the present moment. Especially when done with prayerful awareness, movement becomes medicine for the soul. (Mehling et al., 2011)

As the Beloved, your movement is not a means to earn love. It's a response to it. It's worship. It's a way back into your body, back into your story, and back into the truth that you are already enough already loved already held.

Ask Him:

> "God, how do You want me to move this week?"
> "What does my body need today?"
> "Is this about obedience or control?"

Fitness doesn't have to be complicated.
It just needs to be *consecrated*.
That's where sustainability begins.

Reflection Prompts

1. What season of life am I in right now? What does it demand?

2. Have I been treating fitness as punishment or as partnership?

3. What kind of movement feels life-giving and realistic for me this week?

4. How can I invite God into my fitness rhythm today?

Embodied Prayer

Lord,
Thank You for creating me to move.
Help me stop chasing perfection and start practicing presence.
Give me eyes to see the season I'm in, and wisdom to honor it well.
Teach me rhythms that are sustainable, joyful, and rooted in grace.
Let movement be an overflow of love, not a reaction to shame.
This temple is Yours. This season is Yours.
Strengthen me as I move with You.
In Jesus' name, Amen.

Covered & Held Stillness Practice

Setup:
Sit or lie in a quiet space with your hands resting on your abdomen and chest.

Practice:
Breathe slowly and say:

> *"This is my season. I am allowed to slow down."*

Picture your breath rising and falling like waves.
Feel the pace of your current season not rushing, not resisting just *being*.

Ask: *"Where am I striving when You've invited me to be steady?"*

Close by whispering:

"I am covered. I am held. I am rooted in rhythm."

Movement-Based Exercise
Movement Mapping

Setup:
You'll need a journal or your phone notes + 5–10 minutes of quiet movement.

Practice:

1. **Take a walk, gentle stretch, or body scan**
   Ask yourself: *"How does my body feel today?"*

2. **Record what you notice**:

   - Do you feel tense? Energized? Restless? Calm?

   - What kind of movement feels nourishing today?

3. **Plan your week based on your *season*, not your shame.**

Use the following rhythm as a guide:

Day	Movement Focus	Intention
Monday	Strength	"I build with God."
Tuesday	Mobility / Stretch	"I soften and surrender."
Wednesday	Walk or Cardio Flow	"I move with joy."
Thursday	Rest or Gentle Flow	"I receive recovery."
Friday	Play / Dance / Free	"I delight in my body."
Weekend	Sabbath or Reset	"I am still and loved."

Let the movement match the moment not the pressure.
Ready to put what you've read into practice?
Download the FaithFueled Life App and take your journey deeper. Inside, you'll find guided breath prayers, embodied movement sessions, Scripture meditations, and soul-strengthening practices that bring this book to life. Don't just read about transformation. Live it.
www.tinyurl.com/FAITHFUELEDAPP and begin your journey of becoming the Embodied Beloved.

Chapter 10: From Body Battle to Body Blessing

"Therefore, there is now no condemnation for those who are in Christ Jesus."- Romans 8:1

The Beloved Speaks

"I've spent most of my life at war with my body. Hating it. Criticizing it. Ignoring it. I thought shame would change me, but it only left me feeling numb. Then one day, Coach De's growth work assignment was to look in the mirror and say 'Thank You' instead of hate. That was the beginning. I started blessing my body instead of battling it. I started nourishing it, honoring it, even speaking kindly to it. It felt awkward at first, but now it feels like freedom. I'm not at war anymore. I'm at peace."
— The Beloved

You were never meant to fight your body. You were meant to bless it.

But for many of us, especially women. The relationship with our body has felt like a long, exhausting war. We've starved it into submission, punished it into smaller sizes, and compared it into silence. We've stood in front of mirrors and apologized for it, hidden it behind oversized clothes or perfect photos, and tried to fix it like a problem instead of honoring it as a temple. Somewhere along the way, the body that was knit together by God became the place we poured our shame. We stopped seeing our bodies as holy ground, and started treating them like enemies. But what if your body isn't a battlefield? What if it's a blessing? Even now, even here, even as it aches, stretches, or changes?

For we are not fighting against flesh-and-blood enemies, but against evil rulers and authorities of the unseen world, against mighty powers in this dark world, and against evil spirits in the heavenly places.
Ephesians 6:12

Because our physical and spiritual are not disconnected. We are in a battle constantly and our body,mind and spirit are being attacked all at once. It's a triple threat.

Your body has never been your enemy. "The enemy is the enemy." It has been your witness. Carrying every joy, heartbreak, prayer, and breakthrough. The tension you feel isn't a failure of discipline. It's the grief of disconnection. You were created for union, not war. And the first place of reconnection isn't a new workout or diet. It's truth. You are fearfully and wonderfully made (Psalm 139:14). Not when you get your act together. Not when you lose the weight. Right now. The Creator declared your body very good before you ever tried to fix it. That means your healing doesn't begin in control. It begins in compassion.

Science affirms this sacred truth. The field of psychoneuroimmunology which is the study of how thoughts, emotions, and beliefs affect the body. It reveals that chronic stress and self-criticism dysregulate the nervous system and weaken immune function (Kemeny, 2003). In contrast, practices of self-compassion and embodiment activate the parasympathetic nervous system, helping to restore peace and balance to the body (Porges, 2011). When you approach your body not with judgment, but with gentle curiosity, your physiology shifts. Healing begins. Regulation returns. You no longer live in defense mode. You live from a place of safety, love, and belonging.

Beloved, you don't have to keep fighting. The invitation is to bless your body. To see it not as a project to fix, but as a place where God is present. A dwelling place of glory. A sacred vessel carrying the story of redemption. This isn't just theory. It's the truth of your design, affirmed by Scripture, affirmed by science, and affirmed by the Spirit who lives within you.

The Battle Begins with Belief

Faith is not just the starting point of our salvation. It's the sustaining force of our sanctification. It is the soil from which healing, hope, and holy transformation grow. All throughout the gospels, Jesus honors belief not as intellectual assent, but as embodied trust. Again and again, we see people healed not merely by physical touch, but by the posture of their hearts. "Daughter, your faith has made you well," He says to the woman who risked shame just to touch His robe (Mark 5:34). "Go," He tells the blind man, "your faith has healed you" (Mark 10:52). Faith, in the Kingdom of God, isn't passive. It's participatory.

Even after His resurrection, Jesus met His disciples in their doubt, not with condemnation, but with invitation: "Stop doubting and believe" (John 20:27). Belief wasn't optional. It was essential. It was the bridge between fear and peace, between despair and joy, between sickness and wholeness.

From a neurological standpoint, belief isn't merely spiritual; it's biological. What we believe, we begin to embody. Neuroscience confirms that sustained belief rewires the brain, strengthening the neural pathways associated with hope, gratitude, and resilience. When Scripture calls us to "renew our minds" (Romans 12:2), it's not metaphor it's mechanism. Our faith literally reshapes our brains and, in turn, reshapes our behaviors, our bodies, and the way we live in the world.

But here's the sacred tension: faith isn't always a feeling. It's often a choice to move in the direction of God's promises when your body still carries the tremble of trauma. It's the decision to get low in worship, even when your circumstances shout otherwise. It's the radical act of aligning your mind with the truth of God's Word when your emotions try to drag you back into survival mode.

To be the embodied beloved is to believe even with trembling hands and an aching heart. It's to risk again. To reach again. To say, like the father of the sick child, "I do believe; help my unbelief!" (Mark 9:24). *Remember Chapter 3?* Because belief is not the absence of doubt. It's the refusal to let doubt have the final word.

You didn't enter this world at war with your body. That fracture was learned. It was handed to you in a moment, in a memory, or over time. Sometimes it arrived through a careless comment that stuck like a thorn. Other times through rejection that wrapped itself around your nervous system, whispering that you weren't enough. Maybe it came when the scale dictated your worth more than Scripture ever did. Or when a single image or comparison burned itself into your imagination and redefined your definition of beauty and value. Slowly, quietly, you agreed with a lie that felt like truth.

Because the battle we face in our bodies often begins as a battle in our beliefs.

"If I looked different, I'd be more lovable."

"If I were thinner, God could use me more."

"If I were more disciplined, I'd finally feel worthy."

But here's what's really happening: our brains, wired for survival, latch onto narratives that feel safe. Even if they're not true. According to neuroscience, the stories we rehearse become the neural pathways we default to. Ingrained in our brain and whether they're faulty or not we listen.

If your body has been the scapegoat for your pain, your shame, or your unmet longings, it's not because you're broken. It's because your brain was trying to make sense of suffering the only way it knew how: through control, comparison, or condemnation. Yet none of these beliefs reflect how God sees you. Not one.

You are not the sum of your body parts or the product of your perceived imperfections. You are the Beloved. Fearfully and wonderfully made. Knit together with intention, crowned with glory, and indwelt by the Spirit of the Living God. Your body is not a barrier to God's purpose. It is His chosen dwelling place. The thing is I can tell you this but unless you change the narrative. The belief. Taking captive the old and replacing it with the new. None of this will matter.

To heal your relationship with your body is not vanity. It's spiritual warfare. Because the enemy would love for you to stay distracted by shame instead of present in your purpose.

But you are being invited, right now into a different story. One where love, not lack, is the foundation. One where embodiment is holy, and worth is not earned but received. One where your body is no longer the battleground, but the vessel of blessing. You have to intentionally accept.

Selah Moment: Breath Prayer
Inhale: This body is not my enemy.
Exhale: It is a temple of the Living God.

You Are Not Too Much. You Are Not Not Enough.

God never asked you to be smaller.
He asked you to be surrendered.
The culture might celebrate control, flat stomachs, and "bounce back" culture.
But the Kingdom celebrates *transformation of the heart*.
It honors the unseen. The sacred. The Spirit at work within.

Your stretch marks? Proof of life.
Your thighs? Strong pillars.
Your belly? The place where joy and grief have been carried.
Your skin? Covered by grace.

How to Move from Battle to Blessing

You don't have to like everything about your body to bless it. And you certainly don't have to wait for it to change before honoring what already is. In fact, if you wait to love your body until it meets some ideal, you'll likely never arrive because the measuring stick of cultural worthiness keeps moving. But the truth of your worth in Christ is fixed and eternal.

Blessing your body isn't passivity. It's permission. It's a holy declaration that says:

"Even now, in this shape, in this season, in this struggle, you are worthy of care. You are fearfully and wonderfully made." Psalm 139:14

This isn't self-indulgence. It's spiritual alignment. Blessing is not the same as boasting; it's acknowledgment. It's stepping into agreement with how God sees you, even before you feel it or fully believe it. And this agreement has both spiritual and scientific power.

From a neuroscience perspective, what we say about our bodies reinforces the neural pathways we live from. Words are not neutral they are either constructing patterns of love or reinforcing loops of shame. Repeatedly speaking blessings over your body creates new grooves in the brain, gradually shifting how you perceive yourself, which changes how you treat yourself. Your brain is listening. Your nervous system is responding. Your cells are storing the messages you send.

Spiritually, blessing your body is a return to Eden where humanity walked with God in embodied union, without shame. It's choosing to live as though you are already beloved, already enough, already home.

Try this embodied blessing practice. A sacred reorientation in three simple, intentional steps:

1. Pause and place your hands on your belly.

This is your center. The place your breath expands. The home of your gut instinct, where the vagus nerve branches and healing begins. Say gently but intentionally, "Thank you." Not because it feels perfect, but because this part of you has held so much emotionally, physically, spiritually. Let this be an act of reclaiming your body as a place of compassion, not criticism.

2. Look in the mirror and invite divine perspective.

This is not about rehearsing affirmations detached from reality. This is about realignment. With your eyes locked on your reflection, pray aloud: "God, show me what You see." Wait. Listen. Notice what rises. Maybe it's discomfort. Maybe it's peace. Maybe it's silence. That's okay. The practice itself is forming you. You're creating space for the Spirit to disrupt old lies and sow new truth.

3. Lay down at the end of the day, hand over heart or resting on your side, and whisper,

"This body carried me again today. I bless it." This simple sentence is both recognition and release. You don't have to rehearse every perceived failure of the day. You don't have to punish yourself into change. You can bless your body into becoming.

Because here's the paradox of healing: it often begins the moment we stop fighting our bodies and start partnering with them. The moment we trade hostility for hospitality. The moment we remember that this body isn't a problem to fix. It's a temple to honor, a vessel to steward, a sacred site where the Spirit of God dwells.

You don't have to love every curve, scar, or symptom to treat yourself with sacred kindness.

Start here.

Start with blessing.

Healing from Body Battles
Dr. Emily Falk, a prominent researcher at the intersection of neuroscience, identity, and behavior, has illuminated something Scripture and the Spirit have been whispering all along: what we believe about our bodies shapes our brains, and our lives. Her studies reveal that the narratives we carry about our bodies are not just psychological they're deeply biological.

The words we speak over ourselves, the judgments we silently harbor, and the shame we've inherited don't just float in the air; they settle into the structure of our neural pathways, reinforcing cycles of disconnection and distortion. As Falk puts it, "What we say to ourselves about our bodies. What we believe, what we tell ourselves about how we look and how we ought to look can profoundly change our experience of our own flesh" (Falk, 2014).

I often say, "Be careful what you say to yourself, because you're listening."

Your self-talk isn't just background noise. It's a reflection of your inner alignment. Is it Spirit-led bearing fruit in love, joy, peace, patience, kindness, goodness, faithfulness, gentleness, and self-control (Galatians 5:22–23)? Or is it your flesh speaking marked by anger, jealousy, comparison, and condemnation?

What you whisper to yourself reveals who you're in agreement with: the Holy Spirit or your old survival patterns. Let your words be evidence of the freedom within.

This is not just theory. It's the truth backed by both science and Scripture. Romans 12:2 urges us to be transformed by the renewing of our minds. This renewal isn't merely a spiritual metaphor; it's a neuroplastic process. Our brains are capable of rewiring in response to repeated patterns of thought, attention, and intention. When we stop cursing our bodies and start blessing them, we disrupt old fear-based loops and lay down new neural tracks of love, grace, and peace. We are not merely "thinking positively"; we are realigning with our Creator's original design. A design that calls us very good (Genesis 1:31).

In The Embodied Beloved, we reclaim this truth: that honoring our flesh is not vanity, but obedience. When we bless our bodies, we participate in healing not just emotional, but physical and neurological healing. The Spirit partners with our willingness, and slowly, we become women who no longer war with our bodies but dwell within them as sacred space. We begin to see that the body is not a problem to be fixed but a beloved home to be nurtured, renewed, and reclaimed.

Reflection Prompts
1. What's the earliest memory you have of feeling at war with your body?

2. What beliefs are you still holding about your body that don't align with God's Word?

3. What part of your body needs a blessing today?

4. What does God say about your body that you've struggled to believe?

Embodied Prayer
God,
I've spent so much time battling the body You gave me.
But I'm tired of the war. I want peace.
I want to bless what I've spent years criticizing.
Help me see my body the way You do wonderfully made and deeply loved.
Thank You for creating me with intention.
Forgive me for the times I treated this temple like a problem.
I choose blessing over battle. Gratitude over shame.
Let me walk in the freedom You've already given me.
In Jesus' name, Amen.

Covered & Held Stillness Practice
Bless Your Temple

Setup:
Lie down on your back or sit comfortably.
Place your hands gently over your heart and belly.

Practice:
Take a deep breath and say:

> *"This is my temple. I choose peace, not perfection."*

Feel your breath rise and fall.
With each exhale, imagine releasing any negative beliefs you've carried about your body. Feel the Holy Spirit fill those spaces.

Close with:

> *"I bless this temple. I am at peace."*

Movement-Based Exercise
Body Blessing Flow

Setup:
Find a quiet space. You can stand or sit, depending on what feels right.

Practice:

1. **Reach upward** with arms raised, palms open.
   Say: *"I receive God's truth over my body."*

2. **Slowly bend forward** as if bowing, releasing what you no longer need.
   Say: *"I release shame, control, and comparison."*

3. **Step side to side, softly swaying.**
   Breathe deeply, letting the movement bring release.

Say: *"I bless this body. I honor it with every step."*

4. **Finish with stillness** hands over heart or knees, breathing in gratitude.

Body Blessing Practice: From Battle to Blessing

Posture: Stand barefoot before a mirror. Unclothed if comfortable, or simply place your hands over your heart and belly. Stand tall not in shame, but in sacred attention. Feel the ground beneath your feet. This is holy ground. You are holy ground.

Breath: Inhale slowly through your nose for four counts. Exhale through your mouth for six counts. Do this three times. Let each breath be a gentle invitation to return to your body not to judge it, but to be with it.

Begin the Blessing:
Speak aloud yes, aloud. Your nervous system responds differently when you hear your own voice. Neural pathways of shame begin to weaken when confronted with consistent, compassionate truth.

"Thank you, body.
Thank you for surviving what I thought I had to starve or silence.
Thank you for carrying me through years of shame, through diets, through criticism, through pushing and punishing.
You never gave up on me even when I gave up on you."

Pause. Let those words settle. Let any emotion rise. Tears are welcome. Trembling is healing.

Now gently begin to move your hands over your body wherever healing is needed. Speak a blessing over each part.

"I bless my belly. Not because it is flat, but because it has held sorrow and still breathes life.
I bless my thighs. Not because they are small, but because they are strong and have carried me.
I bless my arms. Not because they are toned, but because they reach, hold, lift, love.
I bless my skin. For holding the story of survival and rebirth."

Scripture Meditation:
"You created my inmost being; You knit me together in my mother's womb. I praise You because I am fearfully and wonderfully made."
—Psalm 139:13–14

Say aloud, even if your voice trembles:

"I am not at war anymore. I am at peace.
I am not ashamed. I am beloved.
I am not fixing myself. I am befriending myself.
My body is no longer my battleground.
It is my blessing."

Close with Prayer:
Jesus, You wore flesh to restore mine. You touched lepers, fed the hungry, wept with the grieving, and rose with scars still showing. Teach me to honor this temple You've entrusted to me not to perform or perfect it, but to dwell in it as You do with gentleness, truth, and grace. Amen.

Chapter 11- What do I do to move? How much? How long? Why?

"Your hands shaped me and made me. You clothed me with skin and flesh and knit me together with bones and sinews." — Job 10:8, 11 (NIV)

The Beloved Speaks

"I used to think exercise was only about weight loss. I chased every new trend HIIT, spin, barre, but I was always exhausted, injured, or frustrated. It wasn't until I worked with Coach De that I began to understand that not all movement is created equal, and that God designed our bodies for more than just the scale. She taught me how to strengthen what was weak, release what was tight, and restore what had been overworked. I didn't need to hustle harder. I needed to move smarter. Lifting weights gave me confidence and stability. Gentle mobility work relieved my joint pain. And walking became my quiet time with God. Now, I don't just move to burn calories. I move to live well, to worship, and to steward this temple I've been given."- The Beloved

Designed to Move

Movement was part of God's original design. Before the fall, Adam and Eve were placed in the garden not just to enjoy it but to work it and take care of it (Genesis 2:15). That Hebrew word for "work," abad, also means to serve and worship. Movement, from the beginning, was a form of stewardship and devotion. God designed the human body to move. Not just occasionally, but consistently, rhythmically, and with variety. Sedentary living is not neutral; it slowly breaks down the very temple we've been called to honor. But movement that is intentional and aligned with God's rhythms can restore us; body, mind, and spirit.

The Science of Sustained Movement

Research confirms what Scripture declares: movement is medicine. Exercise improves nearly every system in the body; muscular, skeletal, cardiovascular, endocrine, lymphatic, and neurological. Here's how:

- Functional Movement improves coordination, balance, posture, and injury prevention. It mimics daily tasks and builds real-life strength (ex: squatting, hinging, pushing, pulling, carrying).

- Strength Training builds lean muscle, improves metabolism, balances hormones, and protects joints. It is essential for both men and women, especially as we age.

- Cardiovascular Training strengthens the heart, enhances endurance, and supports emotional regulation.

- Mobility and Flexibility Work reduces inflammation, promotes recovery, and increases range of motion. Allowing you to move through life with grace and freedom.

- Restorative Movement like walking, stretching, breathwork, and gentle flow yoga supports the parasympathetic nervous system and aids in healing.

Let's not overcomplicate what God made simple. Movement is not optional for thriving. It's essential. Your body was made to move consistently, rhythmically, and with variation. And not just for your muscles, but your mind.

As Caroline Williams writes in *Move: How the New Science of Body Movement Can Set Your Mind Free*,

> "As a result, our biological baseline is to be on our feet, moving and thinking at the same time. If we don't do it, our brains make the sensible decision to save energy by cutting brain capacity. When we get on our feet and move, it primes the brain to be alert and to learn." (Williams, 2021)

Whether you're walking while praying, stretching while reflecting, or strength training while speaking life over your body. Movement sharpens the mind and reawakens the soul. This isn't just self-care. It's stewardship.

Caroline Williams also reminds us,

> "It is entirely possible to use the way we move as a form of self-management for better physical and mental functioning." (Williams, 2021)

This aligns beautifully with what we know in Scripture: we are not meant to live disembodied, numb, or disconnected. We are called to steward our temples (1 Corinthians 6:19–20), to offer our bodies in worship (Romans 12:1), and to let everything that has breath praise the Lord (Psalm 150:6). Movement is both a biological gift and a spiritual discipline.

Selah Moment: Breath Prayer

Inhale: You designed me with a purpose
Exhale: I will move with that purpose
Repeat as you move.

Wonderfully and Uniquely Made: Understanding Your Movement Blueprint

You are not a machine to be programmed. You are a temple to be nourished. There is no one-size-fits-all movement plan because you are a one-of-a-kind creation. Understanding your body's natural tendencies can help you move in ways that honor both your design and your Designer.

Science recognizes three general somatotypes, which are body types that reflect how we store fat, build muscle, and respond to movement. While most people are a blend, knowing your dominant type can help you train more effectively.

1. Ectomorph

- Traits: Long limbs, lean build, difficulty gaining muscle or fat.

- Best Movement: Resistance training with lower volume but heavier loads; focus on building strength and muscle mass with compound lifts. Avoid excessive cardio.

- Why It Matters: Ectomorphs often feel discouraged by slow or minimal physical changes, especially when following high-rep, cardio-heavy routines that don't support their natural design. Prioritizing strength-based workouts and adequate protein intake helps lay a strong, functional foundation. When you're following a plan that doesn't align with your body type, it's easy to feel frustrated by the lack of results. But when you train according to how you were made, you begin to see progress that is both sustainable and empowering.

2. Mesomorph

- **Traits:** Naturally muscular, gains strength easily, athletic build.

- Best Movement: A mix of strength and cardiovascular training; thrives on variety and responds well to progressive overload.

- Why It Matters: Mesomorphs may feel tempted to overtrain. Strategic rest and periodization help them maintain results sustainably.

3. Endomorph

- Traits: Soft, round body type; gains weight easily, especially in the lower body.

- Best Movement: Circuit-style strength training with cardio intervals, walking, and mobility work. Nutritional support is key for hormone and metabolic balance.

- Why It Matters: Endomorphs often carry shame around their weight. But when they stop punishing and start training with wisdom, they unlock powerful endurance and strength.

You are fearfully and wonderfully made (Psalm 139:14), but also purposefully and individually built. Job 10:8 reminds us that our flesh, bones, and sinews are hand-crafted. That includes your metabolism, hormone profile, muscle fiber distribution, and recovery needs. There is freedom in knowing your frame and grace in moving with it not against it.

What Should I Do?
You don't need a gym membership, a six-day split, or the perfect playlist. But you do need movement that:

1. Engages multiple muscle groups

2. Aligns with your season of life and energy levels

3. Builds consistency, not burnout

4. Points you back to the Giver, not the grind

This is what the research supports and the Spirit affirms. A sustainable weekly framework for most women:

Movement Type	Frequency	Duration	Why It Matters
Functional Strength Training	2–3x/week	30–45 minutes/session	Increases muscle, metabolism, and functional capacity
Cardiovascular Movement	2–3x/week	20–40 minutes/session	Supports heart health, endurance, and emotional release
Mobility / Flexibility Work	Daily or 3–5x/week	10–15 minutes/session	Enhances range of motion and reduces chronic pain or tension
Restorative Movement	1–2x/week	15–30 minutes/session	Promotes recovery, lowers cortisol, centers your spirit
Play / Joyful Movement	As often as possible	Any amount	Reconnects you to your body through laughter, leisure, or dance

How Much? How Long? Start Where You Are.

If you're asking, "How much is enough?" you're not alone. But the better question is, what's sustainable in this season? If you're overwhelmed, start with ten minutes. You don't have to overhaul your life to begin honoring your temple. My FaithFueled Life App has many options for a structured way to move. If you need guidance on how to execute movement. It also has daily devotions to keep your mind and spirit focused on the Lord.

Movement isn't a punishment for what you ate or a payment for your worth. It's a powerful act of worship, stewardship, and presence. Every time you rise up and move with intention, you're declaring, "My body is not a burden. It's a vessel of glory."

Why It Matters

Your movement practice isn't just about fitness. It's about freedom. It's about moving because you can, not because you have to. It's about embodying the truth that God gave you a body not just to exist, but to express His love, power, and presence.

Scripture doesn't prescribe workouts, but it gives us a lens through which to view our movement:

- Purpose: "So whether you eat or drink or whatever you do, do it all for the glory of God." (1 Corinthians 10:31)

- Stewardship: "Do you not know that your bodies are temples of the Holy Spirit... Therefore honor God with your bodies." (1 Corinthians 6:19–20)

- Joy: "Let everything that has breath praise the Lord." (Psalm 150:6)
  You don't have to chase the world's trends to live well. You just need to move with intention, consistency, and grace.

Reflection Prompts

1. How have you viewed movement in the past? Has it been punishment, performance, or partnership with God?

2. What lies have you believed about your body's ability to move?

3. Which types of movement do you most enjoy, and which have you avoided?

4. How might understanding your unique body type (somatotype) shift your approach to movement?

5. What would it look like to invite the Holy Spirit into your movement routines?

Embodied Prayer

Father God,
Thank You for creating my body with intention and care.
You knit me together with sinews, bones, and breath.
Forgive me for every time I've despised or neglected this body. This temple. I want to move not for approval or appearance, but for stewardship and joy.
Renew my mind around what movement means.

Let it become worship, not worry.
Presence, not punishment.
Help me to listen to what my body needs and to trust You with how it changes.
Make me strong, Lord.
Not just physically, but spiritually.
As I stretch, strengthen, and move, may Your Spirit move through me.
In Jesus' name, Amen.

Covered & Held Stillness Practice

Theme: Movement Begins in Stillness

Posture: Seated or lying down, spine neutral, hands resting on your lower belly.

Cue: Begin with deep, diaphragmatic breaths. Feel the rise and fall of your abdomen. As you inhale, envision God's hands shaping your frame. As you exhale, imagine Him holding you still reminding you that movement doesn't begin in chaos. It begins in His calm.

Prompt: Silently speak over yourself:

> "I am not behind. I am not broken. My body is the home God has chosen. I am safe to move at the pace of grace."

Duration: 5–7 minutes of intentional stillness.

Movement-Based Practice

Theme: Move in the Manner You Were Made

Warm-Up (3–5 min):

- Cat-Cow (spinal mobility)
- Air squats
- Arm circles
- Ankle rolls

Strength Circuit (repeat 2x):

- Bodyweight or weighted squats – 10 reps
- Modified pushups or wall pushups – 10 reps
- Bent-over rows (bands or dumbbells) – 10 reps
- Glute bridges – 10 reps
- Bird-Dogs – 10 reps per side

Cool Down + Stretch (3–5 min):

- Forward fold
- Lunge with twist
- Seated spinal twist
- Child's Pose
- Final breath prayer

This movement isn't to prove anything. It's to honor everything God has given you. Listen to your body. Rest when needed. Celebrate what moves.

Part 4: Nourishment and Freedom

Slowing Down to Savor God's Provision

You were created to feast, to rest, to live at God's pace.

This part of the journey invites you to lay down hurry, hustle, and frantic control. You'll learn the holy rhythms of nourishment where food becomes a gift, not a battleground, and your life moves to the cadence of daily grace.

Chapter 12: Nourish to Flourish Rebuilding Your Relationship with Food

*Why spend money on what is not bread,
and your labor on what does not satisfy?
Listen, listen to me, and eat what is good,
and you will delight in the richest of fare.*
-Isaiah 55:2

The Beloved Speaks

"I didn't realize how deeply food ruled me. I wasn't just hungry for nourishment. I was hungry for control, for comfort, for love. I used to either punish myself with restriction or numb myself with bingeing. But when I started seeing food as a gift instead of a threat, everything began to change. Now, eating is an act of worship. I bless my meals. I listen to my body. And for the first time, I feel free."
— The Beloved

Food was never meant to be a battlefield. But for many of us, our relationship with food is layered with fear, shame, guilt, rules, overwhelm and confusion. It's not just about what we eat.

Our relationship with food doesn't begin in the kitchen. It starts at birth. Before we ever took a step or spoke a word, we cried, and someone offered us a bottle or a breast, not always knowing what we truly needed. Sometimes we were tired. Sometimes we were overstimulated. Sometimes we just needed to be held. But nourishment became a stand-in for comfort, quiet, and connection.

From our very first breath, food was more than fuel. It became emotional. And for many of us, it still is.

Science shows that the early neural pathways connecting the hypothalamus (which regulates hunger) and the limbic system (which processes emotion) get reinforced over time. So when we're stressed, scared, lonely, or tired, we don't just feel those emotions; we crave. Not because we're weak, but because our brain learned that food fixes feelings, even when it doesn't.

And when you trace it all the way back to Genesis, the very first sin? It involved food. Not because the fruit was magical, but because it represented desire, control, identity, and distrust in God's goodness.

We've been trying to feed soul hunger with physical solutions ever since. So when my clients come to me women of faith, committed to honoring God with their bodies but frustrated by the battle with food. It's not just about macros or meal plans. It's about beliefs.

Many of my clients' deepest struggles with food are rooted in distorted beliefs. Beliefs about their worth. Their body. God's provision. And whether or not they're truly allowed to be nourished and satisfied.

That's why healing your relationship with food isn't just physical it's spiritual, emotional, and neurological.
And that healing begins when we bring those hidden beliefs into the light of God's truth. It's about what we believe food says about us:

That we're good if we restrict.

Weak if we indulge.
Out of control if we enjoy it too much.
More disciplined if we ignore our hunger.
But what if nourishing your body isn't about willpower or punishment?
What if it's a form of worship?

Your beliefs are not just thoughts you think. They are the way you operate in the world. They shape your choices, your habits, your vision of what's possible. And at the same time, they hold the key to your freedom. Renew your beliefs, and you renew your life.

God Cares About Your Nourishment

From the very beginning, God has revealed Himself as a God who feeds. Nourishment is not an afterthought to Him. It is woven into the very fabric of His relationship with His people. In the wilderness, after delivering the Israelites from slavery, He provided manna, bread from heaven, one day at a time (Exodus 16). He did not rain down a lifetime supply at once. He gave only enough for each day, teaching His people that physical nourishment was inseparable from spiritual dependence. They could not stockpile security; they had to trust the Giver daily. In the act of feeding, God was shaping their hearts, inviting them to surrender their fear, their striving, and their self-reliance in exchange for a living trust in His provision.

This pattern of sacred nourishment continues in the life of Jesus. When crowds gathered, hungry not only for His words but weary in body, Jesus did not send them away. He took the little that was available. Five loaves and two fishes, and blessed it, broke it, and multiplied it until all were satisfied, with baskets left over (Matthew 14:13–21). In feeding the multitudes, Jesus was not merely meeting a need; He was embodying the compassion of the Father. His miracles around food, simple, abundant, and tender, revealed that God cares for the whole person: body, mind, and spirit. Hunger was not treated as a weakness to be scorned, but as a doorway through which God's abundance and compassion could be revealed.

Throughout Scripture, meals hold deep covenantal meaning. Abraham welcomed divine visitors by preparing a feast, and through that meal, he received the promise of a son (Genesis 18). The Passover meal was instituted to mark the deliverance of God's people from death and slavery, a sacred remembering to be repeated across generations (Exodus 12).

In the New Testament, the breaking of bread became an act of fellowship and remembrance. Most poignantly in the Last Supper, where Jesus took bread and wine, blessed them, and instituted a new covenant sealed by His own body and blood (Luke 22:19–20). And the story is not yet complete.

Revelation points us to a future feast. The Marriage Supper of the Lamb where all who belong to Christ will gather in joy and celebration (Revelation 19:9).

Eating, then, is not separate from the sacred. It can be a sacred act itself. A table can be an altar. A meal can be a testimony.

"So whether you eat or drink or whatever you do, do it all for the glory of God." -1 Corinthians 10:31, NIV

When we nourish ourselves well, we are participating in this sacred story. To nourish well means to care for your body in alignment with your worth, not your weight.

It means choosing to eat from a place of connection, not disconnection, not restriction, not fear, not fixation. It means honoring hunger as a God-given messenger, not something to fear, suppress, or fight against, but something to listen to with curiosity and trust. It means receiving food as a provision, not a punishment; as a blessing, not a burden.

Nourishing well is an embodied act of trust. It is acknowledging that your needs are not a nuisance to God but an invitation to experience His care. It is recognizing that your body is fearfully and wonderfully made (Psalm 139:14). It is not a project to fix or an ornament to display, but a living temple in which the Spirit of God dwells (1 Corinthians 6:19–20).

When we listen to our bodies with grace instead of condemnation, we echo the truth that God Himself listens to us with grace. When we eat from a place of freedom, we reflect the abundant life Christ came to give (John 10:10).

To nourish well is to remember:
You are not what you eat.
You are not what you weigh.
You are not how tightly you can control your cravings or how perfectly you can perform a diet.
You are the beloved.
You are fed.
You are the invited guest at the table of abundance. Not because you earned a seat, but because grace made a way.

To nourish well is to let your eating ordinary and sacred become a daily act of worship, trust, and embodied faith.
It looks like freedom, not fixation.
It feels like care, not punishment.

It sounds like the gentle whisper of a Good Shepherd saying, "Come, and be filled."

Selah Moment: Breath Prayer
Inhale: I am allowed to be nourished.
Exhale: I receive food as a gift, not a guilt.

The Science of Nourishment + Emotion
Your relationship with food isn't just about what you know; it's also about how your body and heart are carrying stress and emotion. Chronic stress elevates cortisol, which can increase cravings for sugar, fat, and salt as your body seeks comfort and regulation (Tomiyama et al., 2011). The gut-brain axis shows how closely our emotional health and digestion are linked. What we eat can influence our mood, and how we feel can shape how we nourish ourselves (Mayer et al., 2015).

When you find yourself stuck in patterns like restricting and bingeing, it's not because you're broken or undisciplined. It's often your body's way of coping with internal chaos. But God does not stand far off when you struggle.

Scripture reminds us, *"The Lord is close to the brokenhearted and saves those who are crushed in spirit"* (Psalm 34:18, NIV).

What does that mean? You're not broken. You're responding to internal chaos with external control. But healing is possible. And it starts with listening to your body with curiosity and grace.

"He makes me lie down in green pastures, He leads me beside quiet waters, He restores my soul." — Psalm 23:2–3

God is not just interested in what you eat. He's concerned with why you eat, how you feel when you eat, and what you believe about your body while doing it.

Releasing Shame Around Food

Let's dismantle the lie that your worth is tied to your willpower.
You are not holier when you skip meals.
You are not more loved when you eat less.
You are not more disciplined when you silence hunger.

God designed your body with hunger cues, satisfaction signals, and cravings that are not sinful; they are informational. They are invitations to tune in, not shut down.

And if you've struggled with emotional eating, bingeing, or control, let me say this:
You're not failing.
You're protecting something tender.
But now it's safe to heal.

From Control to Communion

One of the enemy's greatest tactics is to turn something sacred, like eating, into a source of torment. But Jesus came to turn every table of shame into a feast of grace.

What if your next meal became a moment of communion? What if you blessed your food, invited God into the process, and received nourishment with joy?

This is not about perfection. It's about connection.

"Taste and see that the Lord is good." — Psalm 34:8

Reflection Prompts

1. What messages have I received about food and my worth?

2. How has shame shaped my eating habits or hunger cues?

3. What would it look like to eat in a way that honors both God and my body?

Embodied Prayer

Lord,
Thank You for the gift of nourishment.
Forgive me for the ways I've used food to hide, to punish, or to prove something.
Heal the places where fear has shaped my appetite.
Help me to eat in alignment with grace, not guilt.
Restore my hunger cues, my trust in my body, and my ability to receive without fear.
I bless my meals. I bless my body. I bless this journey.

In Jesus' name, Amen.

Covered & Held Stillness Practice
Setup:
Sit comfortably or lie down in stillness.
Place your hands palm-up over your lap or resting over your heart and belly.

Begin:
Breathe in deeply through your nose.
As you exhale, whisper or think: "I let it go."
Picture the heaviness of resentment, self-blame, or betrayal falling off of your shoulders, hips, and chest.
Feel the ground holding you as God holds your story.
You don't have to figure out how to forgive fully you just have to be willing.
Visualize the weight of unforgiveness as a heavy cloak sliding off your back.

"Come to Me, all who are weary and burdened, and I will give you rest." — Matthew 11:28

Close by saying:
"Jesus, I release what was never mine to carry."
Rest here as long as needed.

Movement-Based Exercise: Forgiveness Flow
Setup:
Stand in a grounded stance. Feet hip-width apart, soft knees, relaxed arms.

Practice:
Begin by gently shaking out your hands, arms, and shoulders.

Let it be messy, loose, and unstructured. This isn't a performance it's release.
Say: "I don't need to hold this anymore."

Bring your arms overhead in a big inhale, reaching tall.

Exhale as you sweep your arms down and bow slightly, like laying something at Jesus' feet.

Say: "I lay it down."

Repeat 3–5 times, visualizing the names, memories, or burdens you are surrendering with each movement.

End by standing still, placing one hand over your heart and one over your belly.
Say: "I am free. I am forgiven. I am the Beloved."

Ready to put what you've read into practice?
Download the FaithFueled Life App and take your journey deeper. Inside, you'll find guided breath prayers, embodied movement sessions, Scripture meditations, and soul-strengthening practices that bring this book to life. Whether you're seeking stillness, strength, or spiritual renewal, the app gives you real-time tools to embody your faith and steward your temple; anytime, anywhere.

Don't just read about transformation. Live it.
www.tinyurl.com/FAITHFUELEDAPP and begin your journey of becoming the Embodied Beloved.

Chapter 13: Fed by Grace, Not by Guilt

You, my brothers and sisters, were called to be free. But do not use your freedom to indulge the flesh[a]; rather, serve one another humbly in love.- Galatians 5:13

The Beloved Speaks

"I used to think every bite was a test, and I kept failing. I lived by food rules and shame spirals. If I ate 'clean,' I was proud. If I slipped, I punished myself. But I was never at peace. Then Coach De said, 'Fed by grace, not by guilt.' It unraveled me. Slowly, I started inviting God to the table. I stopped counting calories and started counting on Him. Food stopped being my boss and became a place of worship, rest, and freedom." — The Beloved

We were never created to worship at the altar of food nor to tremble in fear before it. And yet, so many of us have been held hostage by its promises, its punishments, its power. Somewhere along the journey, food stopped being a gift and became a god. We began bowing to cravings, obsessing over numbers, moralizing our meals, and measuring our worth by what we ate or didn't eat. For years, we've been stuck in a tug-of-war with control swinging between restriction that leaves us empty and rebellion that leaves us ashamed. We've handed food the keys to our joy, our identity, even our peace.

Chronic stress around eating wires the brain into survival pathways, reducing access to the prefrontal cortex. Where discernment, self-control, and spiritual reflection dwell. It's no wonder so many of us feel like we're constantly failing. We've been trying to manage a spiritual stronghold with worldly willpower.

The Problem Isn't Food. It's the Fear Around It.

Food was meant to nourish, to delight, even to connect us to the earth, to one another, to the provision of our Creator. But for many of us, it has become something else entirely. For some, food is a coping mechanism: a quiet comfort in the chaos. For others, it's a battleground, where the body is punished in the name of control. And for so many of us, it's both an exhausting cycle of craving and control, numbing and regret, where no meal feels neutral and no hunger feels holy.

We eat not just from our stomachs but from our stories from the wounds we haven't healed, the lies we've believed, and the longings we've tried to silence. Food is necessary for life, yes, but when our relationship with it is disordered, it becomes a stronghold in the spirit. Not because of what's on the plate, but because of what's happening in the heart.

For much of my life, food wasn't just fuel. It was a fixation. As a self-proclaimed food fixator, I spent years obsessing over what I would eat, what I wouldn't eat, and what I felt guilty about eating. There was a season when the list of foods I would eat was painfully shorter than the list I claimed I "couldn't." Not because my body was incapable of handling them, but because fear had taken over my plate.

To be clear, I do have a very real allergy to wheat. But beyond that, I started labeling things like soy, corn, and sugar as intolerant not because my body rejected them, but because my need for control did. Control disguised itself as wellness, and restriction became a badge I wore to prove I was disciplined. When in reality, I was just desperate to feel safe. Food rules gave me a false sense of order when everything inside me felt chaotic.

Sometimes, that obsession looked like discipline meticulously planned meals weighed out to the gram, "clean" eating, and the illusion of control. Other times, it looked like cravings that consumed me, where the desire for comfort drowned out my clarity. I ate so fast I couldn't feel fullness just the ache of emptiness I was trying to silence. Continuing to eat past satisfaction, past discomfort because I wasn't hungry for food. I was hungry for peace. Whether health-conscious or craving-conscious, I've bowed to food in both directions: restriction and rebellion or obsession and neglect.

In the seasons when life felt chaotic or uncertain, I didn't always run to God. I ran to food. Or more accurately, I ran to the control that food offered me. When everything else felt unpredictable, food gave me a script to follow something to track, something to manipulate, something I could master. It became my coping mechanism, my comfort, my counterfeit god. And that's the dangerous part. When I took my eyes off Christ and tried to manage life on my own, food quietly climbed onto the throne of my heart.

But food was never meant to bear that weight. What I've come to understand, through Scripture and science alike, is that our relationship with food reveals so much more than our preferences. It reveals our posture.

1 Corinthians 6:12 warns us: *"'Everything is permissible,' but not everything is beneficial. 'Everything is permissible,' but I will not be mastered by anything."*

Food itself isn't the problem. It's the role we allow it to play. When food becomes the master and we, its servant, our souls begin to suffer. The neural grooves of obsession and avoidance deepen, and our nervous systems remain stuck in survival.

Beloved, you are not what you eat. You are not what you restrict. You are not what you crave. You are not a number on a scale or a label on a package. You are the Beloved of God, designed to be nourished body and spirit by His presence, not enslaved by patterns of control.

Healing begins when we bring even this our fixation, our failures, our food stories to the feet of Jesus. That's where transformation begins. Not in a new plan, but in a surrendered heart.

Please hear and receive this: food was never meant to be the boss of your body. Christ is. And He came not to impose more rules, but to set captives free. The table was always meant to be a place of communion, not control. A space to remember God's provision, not to punish your body.

It's time to break the stronghold.

Through the renewing of your mind and the healing of your nervous system, you can return to food as it was intended: a means of nourishment, an expression of care, a practice of grace. Not a battleground. Not a measuring stick. And definitely not your master.

You are not what you eat. You are who He says you are: chosen, cherished, and completely free.

Selah Moment: Breath Prayer

Inhale: I am fed by grace.
Exhale: Not by guilt.
Repeat three times before meals or when food anxiety surfaces.

How Food Becomes a Stronghold

Food is not just about nutrition. It's also about narrative. And for many of us, the story we've been telling ourselves about food is laced with fear, shame, and control. It begins subtly. A hard day turns into a handful of something sweet to take the edge off. A stressful week ends in a cycle of overeating, followed by the familiar voice of guilt. Or maybe it shows up in the opposite direction rigid control masked as "discipline," where food is weighed, measured, and moralized.

In many churches today, food has become the only culturally acceptable coping mechanism cloaked in celebration. We gather in fellowship halls and Bible studies, offering sugar-laden treats and comfort foods as a sign of welcome.

But what if without knowing it becomes a stumbling block? While no one would dare pass around a cigarette tray or pour a round of shots before prayer, we freely and frequently offer what some of our sisters are actively trying to surrender. The potluck table, meant to foster community, can quietly stir up shame, compulsion, or deep spiritual grief for the woman fighting to break free from food as a stronghold. Or maybe it was just like that for me in my own struggles.

This isn't about demonizing food. God made it good. But when our gatherings unknowingly become places of temptation rather than healing, it reveals something deeper: a collective lack of awareness of how trauma and addiction can manifest through what we consume. Neurologically, the brain responds to sugar, processed carbs, and fatty comfort foods with the same dopamine surge as drugs and alcohol. And when those foods are tied to emotional memory grief, celebration, childhood pain they don't just nourish the body. They become numbing agents, masks for unhealed wounds.

Theologically, we're invited into freedom, not bondage (Galatians 5:1). Yet when we fail to recognize that food can function as a false refuge a socially sanctioned idol we miss an opportunity to disciple one another more deeply. We miss a chance to become communities of true healing, where we feast not to forget, but to remember: the goodness of God, the grace that sustains, and the presence of Christ at every table.

In the Body of Christ, let us not unintentionally reinforce the very chains our sisters are trying to break. Let us serve food with sensitivity, offer alternatives with love, and create space where no one has to choose between fitting in and staying free.

This is how food becomes a stronghold. Not just by what's on our plates, but by what takes up residence in our hearts and minds.

When our emotions dictate what, when, or how we eat, we're no longer nourishing our bodies we're negotiating with them. When guilt, fear, or shame follow every meal, our nervous systems stay trapped in a feedback loop of self-condemnation, and our bodies bear the weight of chronic stress.

Neuroscience tells us that these emotional stressors, especially when habitual, dysregulate the limbic system and reinforce maladaptive patterns meaning the more we associate food with punishment or performance, the more disconnected we become from true hunger and fullness cues.

When food becomes a reward for "being good," an escape from feeling too much, or a punishment for not measuring up, it begins to occupy a spiritual space it was never meant to hold. Even "clean eating" when rooted in fear instead of freedom can become a new form of legalism. What begins as a desire for health can quietly morph into an identity built on avoidance, rigidity, and silent shame.

This isn't about willpower.

It's about worship.

It's about what holds authority in your mind and shapes your daily decisions. Is it grace or is it guilt? Are your food choices born from love and stewardship, or from fear and striving?

Romans 12:1 calls us to *offer our bodies as living sacrifices, holy and pleasing to God this is our spiritual act of worship.*

Not just in church, but in the kitchen. At the table. In the choices we make with open hands and surrendered hearts.

Beloved, the question isn't just "What are you eating?" It's "What's eating you?" What narrative is shaping your relationship with food? What voice are you listening to shame, scarcity, or the Shepherd?

Healing begins when we bring even this stronghold into the light, and surrender it at the feet of Jesus.

The Neuroscience of Food and Emotional Attachment

Neuroscientist Dr. Caroline Leaf explains that our thoughts especially the ones we rehearse over and over carve literal pathways in our brain's structure (Leaf, 2013). Like trails etched into soil by repeated footsteps, these neural pathways become familiar routes the mind returns to. So if our daily inner dialogue around food is marked by guilt, shame, or the need for control, our brains begin to default to those emotions. What was once a passing thought becomes a pattern. And that pattern? It begins to shape our entire relationship with nourishment.

But the story doesn't end there. Our God-designed brains were created with the capacity to change. Neuroplasticity is not just a scientific phenomenon. It's a reflection of divine mercy built into our biology. It means that no thought pattern is permanent. It also reiterates the deep connection of body, mind and spirit. No narrative is too embedded to be rewritten. With every intentional act every moment we choose grace over guilt, every meal approached with reverence instead of restriction, every breath taken in awareness rather than anxiety. We begin to forge new pathways. Gentler ones. Truer ones. This is how freedom begins.

When we eat not to earn our worth but to honor the gift of life we've been given. When we no longer punish the body but partner with it as a vessel of the Spirit. When meals become sacred space instead of battlegrounds. These aren't just behavior shifts. They are belief shifts. They are acts of embodied renewal.

You are not stuck. You are being re-formed mind, body, and spirit by the One who made you. And in this holy re-patterning, grace is not a distant hope. It becomes your daily guide.

The Scroll That's Shaping Our Plates

We are the most nutritionally informed generation in human history, and somehow, still one of the most disoriented. With every scroll, swipe, and sound bite, we're met with a new gospel of food: cut the carbs, count the macros, skip the breakfast, drink the celery juice, eat intuitively, but only within rules someone else made. Fast for 16 hours, feast like a caveman, fear seed oils, follow your blood type, suppress your appetite, or eat every two hours to keep it steady. One scroll and we're left spiritually hungry and biologically confused.

What's happening here isn't just about trends. It's about formation. Every algorithm we engage with is subtly catechizing us. Every "what I eat in a day" video is a liturgy. Every before-and-after photo is a promise of salvation through self-denial, discipline, or superfoods. And the truth is, our nervous systems weren't built to carry this much input.

Research in cognitive overload shows that the brain, when bombarded with conflicting information, defaults into decision fatigue shutting down discernment and ramping up anxiety. Our bodies internalize this stress, and we wonder why we feel so out of control when it comes to food.

Social media has become our modern food law, and influencers our digital high priests. We no longer pause to ask, "Lord, what would You have me eat today to honor the body You gave me?" Instead, we frantically ask, "What are they eating? And how can I control myself enough to do the same?" We've traded the quiet guidance of the Spirit for the noise of the scroll.

But the Word of God has already spoken. In Genesis 1:29, God declares, *"Then God said, "I give you every seed-bearing plant on the face of the whole earth and every tree that has fruit with seed in it. They will be yours for food."*

In Eden, nourishment was whole. Simple. Given. Not tracked, filtered, or idolized just received. God's design for eating was never about aesthetic outcomes or public approval. It was about provision, relationship, and dependence.

The theology of food in Scripture doesn't lead us into obsession or shame. It calls us into stewardship and trust. It reminds us that food is not a performance. It's a provision sometimes a celebration but not a limitation. The gospel doesn't begin with a diet plan, but with a table. And at that table sits the God who says, "Taste and see that the Lord is good" (Psalm 34:8). Not, "Taste and track." Not, "Taste and judge." But taste and see with wonder, with gratitude, with humility.

When we reclaim eating as an embodied act of worship rather than a performance of willpower, we can stop striving to "fix" our bodies and start honoring them. We can stop following the feed and start following the Shepherd. And in that shift, food becomes what it was always meant to be: a daily encounter with the goodness of God.

From Legalism to Liberty

> *"So whether you eat or drink or whatever you do, do it all for the glory of God."* — 1 Corinthians 10:31 (NIV)

> *"Man does not live on bread alone, but on every word that comes from the mouth of God."* — Matthew 4:4 (NIV)

> *"Taste and see that the Lord is good…"* — Psalm 34:8 (NIV)

God created food for nourishment, joy, and connection. It was never meant to be feared or idolized.

You don't need food rules.
You need *Holy Spirit wisdom*.

You don't need to count calories.
You need to *count on God*.

You don't need another detox.
You need to *detox the guilt* that's followed every bite.

Reflection Prompts

1. In what ways has food had power over you emotionally or spiritually?

2. What food beliefs have shaped your body image or self-worth?

3. What would it look like to eat in peace with Jesus at the table?

4. Where do you need more grace in your relationship with food?

Embodied Prayer

Father God,
You are the Bread of Life.
I confess that I've let food define me, control me, shame me.
But You never asked that of me.
You invited me to come and be filled. To taste and see Your goodness.
Help me break free from guilt, fear, and perfectionism around food.
Renew my mind. Rewire my habits.
Teach me to eat with intention, with peace, and in Your presence.
Let every bite become a reminder of Your provision and love.
In Jesus' name, Amen.

Covered & Held Stillness Practice
Sit at the Table

Setup:
Sit at your kitchen table or floor, cross-legged. Close your eyes and rest your hands on your lap.

Practice:
Imagine Jesus sitting across from you at the table.
There is no judgment in His eyes. Only joy. Only peace.

Picture Him breaking bread. He blesses it.
Then He looks at you not your plate, not your body and says:

> *"You are welcome here. Eat in peace."*

Breathe slowly.
Say aloud or silently:

> *"I am not what I eat. I am loved, chosen, and free."*

Movement-Based Exercise
Nourishment Walk

Setup:
After a meal, go for a gentle 10–15 minute walk.

Practice:
With every step, reflect on how that meal served you:

- What did it provide your body?
- How did it taste?
- Did it nourish your soul?

Say aloud or silently as you walk:

> "Thank You, God, for this nourishment."
> "I am at peace with how I care for myself."

Let your movement be your digestion. Let your walk be your worship.

Ready to put what you've read into practice?
Download the FaithFueled Life App and take your journey deeper. Inside, you'll find guided breath prayers, embodied movement sessions, Scripture meditations, and soul-strengthening practices that bring this book to life. Whether you're seeking stillness, strength, or spiritual renewal, the app gives you real-time tools to embody your faith and steward your temple, anytime, anywhere.

Don't just read about transformation. Live it.
www.tinyurl.com/FAITHFUELEDAPP and begin your journey of becoming the Embodied Beloved.

Chapter 14: Satisfy and Sustain

*The righteous eat to their hearts' content,
but the stomach of the wicked goes hungry.* -Proverbs 13:25

The Beloved Speaks

"I used to follow every food trend, every diet rule, every voice but my own. I didn't trust my body. I barely even listened to it. I was always hungry for something, but it wasn't always food. Coach De asked our group to ask the Holy Spirit, "What do we really need?" when going for a treat or a snack. One day, I paused mid-bite and asked, 'Holy Spirit, what do I really need right now?' And everything changed. I started slowing down. Tuning in. Praying before I plated. I'm learning to eat with God, not against myself."
— The Beloved

We were not just created to eat mindfully. We were created to eat prayerfully. God, in His infinite wisdom, designed our bodies with intricate systems that speak to us daily: hunger cues, satiety signals, hormones that whisper when we need nourishment and when we've had enough. And beyond biology, He placed His very Spirit within us to help guide every area of our lives including the table.

Yet somewhere along the way, we began trusting trends more than Truth. We traded discernment for diets and holy rhythms for rigid rules. We started outsourcing our authority first to magazines, then to macros, and now to influencers with no credentials but plenty of followers. Like social media, intuitive eating can become distorted watered down, co-opted, and confusing. But at its root, when rightly ordered, it reflects something sacred, sustainable and steadfast.

Intuitive, Spirit-led eating isn't about impulsivity or indulgence. It's not an excuse to eat without intention. It's a holy invitation back to connection. Connection to the body God knit together in your mother's womb. Connection to the gentle, healing wisdom of the Holy Spirit. And connection to the daily grace of choosing what is nourishing not just physically, but emotionally and spiritually too. And grace is not permission to do what you please. Its a posture check of "Where are you?" and "Where should you be?"

For the grace of God has appeared that offers salvation to all people. It teaches us to say "No" to ungodliness and worldly passions, and to live self-controlled, upright and godly lives in this present age, Titus 2:11-12

You don't need more restriction. What your soul longs for is reconnection. You don't need another rule about what not to eat. You need rhythms of communion. Daily moments of attunement, where you pause, breathe, and ask, "Holy Spirit, what do I need right now? How can I honor You with this choice?"

This is what it means to reclaim eating as worship. This is the difference between legalism and liberation, between striving and surrender. This is what happens when your meals become altars.

What Is Intuitive Eating?

Intuitive eating is a non-diet approach rooted in tuning into your body's God-designed cues for hunger, satisfaction, and fullness.

It's not reckless eating. It's *relational* eating between you, your body, and God. It's not permission to indulge every craving. It's permission to *trust* that God designed your body to know what it needs, and to listen.

When paired with the voice of the Holy Spirit, intuitive eating becomes a holy partnership. Eating becomes worship. Nourishment becomes an act of faith.

Science is finally catching up to what the Spirit has always whispered: we were created not just to eat, but to trust the sacred intelligence God wove into our bodies. Intuitive eating, when rooted in the Spirit and not the self alone, becomes a holy act of listening and honoring the temple God has entrusted to us.

Research affirms what Scripture implies: freedom leads to flourishing. Studies show that intuitive eating is associated with significantly lower rates of disordered eating and body dissatisfaction (Tylka & Kroon Van Diest, 2013). When we stop fighting our bodies and start listening to them with curiosity and compassion, we begin to reflect the peace of the One who made us.

This way of eating also nurtures our emotional and physiological well-being. Emotional resilience and positive body image increase (Bruce & Ricciardelli, 2016), while cortisol levels the hormone tied to chronic stress decrease. Mindful, non-restrictive eating has even been shown to support healthier digestion and metabolic balance (Wansink, 2010). In short: our nervous systems thrive in the presence of grace, not guilt.

Your body was designed for trust. Designed to send signals that guide you, not punish you. Designed to be nourished, restored, and inhabited not managed like a project or feared like an enemy. God didn't create your body to live under the tyranny of chronic stress, shame, or striving.

You are invited to return not just to your hunger cues, but to the One who created them. This is not indulgence. This is embodiment. It's a holy reclamation of your God-given wisdom to eat, digest, and delight in the gift of food without fear.

Selah Moment: Breath Prayer
Inhale: I am nourished by You.
Exhale: I am sustained by You.
Pray this before meals, and during fasting windows.

What Scripture Says About Spirit-Led Eating
Spirit-led eating is not a modern wellness trend. It's a return to an ancient, biblical way of living: one where every part of us, including how we eat, is submitted to the Lordship of Christ. Scripture doesn't offer meal plans or macros, but it does offer principles that guide us back to the table with reverence, freedom, and wisdom.

1. God created eating as good and purposeful.

From the beginning, food was a gift. In (Genesis 1:29) Provision was woven into creation. Eating was not a source of shame or struggle, but of delight and communion. Even after the fall, God continued to meet people in their hunger (Exodus 16, 1 Kings 19) and use food as a sign of His faithfulness.

2. Spirit-led eating involves self-control not self-condemnation.

Galatians 5:22–23 lists self-control as a fruit of the Spirit, not a force of willpower. It's also the last fruit of the Spirit in order. This isn't about dieting or denying our God-given needs. It's about receiving nourishment with wisdom, listening to our bodies with grace, and honoring the temple we've been given (1 Corinthians 6:19–20). Spirit-led self-control is compassionate, not punishing. It says, *"God, help me to steward this moment with love."*

3. Food is never meant to be a god.

Philippians 3:19 warns of those *"whose god is their stomach."* That verse isn't just about overindulgence. It's about disordered worship. When food becomes a place we run to for comfort, control, or identity, it reveals that our hearts are hungry for something deeper. Spirit-led eating reorients us: we eat from satisfaction in Christ, not in pursuit of it.

4. Eating can be an act of worship.

"So whether you eat or drink or whatever you do, do it all for the glory of God." (1 Corinthians 10:31) This verse reframes every meal. Eating isn't just physical. It's spiritual. Every bite can become a moment of gratitude, presence, and embodied praise. Spirit-led eating isn't about rules. It's about rhythm. Not about guilt, but grace. A way of saying with our forks and knives: "God, I trust You, even here."

5. Freedom in Christ includes freedom at the table.

Romans 14 and Colossians 2 remind us not to let anyone judge us by what we eat or don't eat. The gospel frees us from food laws and invites us into wisdom. Spirit-led eating is marked by both discernment and liberty guided by the Spirit, not enslaved by shame or cultural food rules. In the kingdom of God, food is not forbidden, it is redeemed. And eating, when led by the Spirit, becomes an act of worship, wisdom, and deep belonging.

Fasting: Reconnecting Mind, Body, and Spirit

Only 2% of Christians practice fasting today (Barna Research, 2020). Perhaps that's because fasting has been misrepresented. Reduced to a religious performance, a diet in disguise, or a self-inflicted punishment to prove devotion. But fasting was never meant to be any of that.

Fasting isn't starvation. It's not willpower cloaked in shame. It's not another rung on the spiritual ladder to earn love that's already been lavished on us. Fasting is a holy invitation, not to reject the body, but to return to it. To remember we are not ruled by our appetites. We are led by the Spirit.

Biblical fasting is a posture of surrender. A sacred pause. A clarifying act of embodied worship. When you fast, you aren't just abstaining from food. You are intentionally interrupting the default mode of disconnection. You are carving out space to listen, to feel, to reorient. Fasting gently exposes the places where we've numbed with nourishment instead of seeking the Bread of Life.

This isn't about depriving the body to hate it. It's about emptying so we can be filled. It's about aligning with the ancient words of Jesus, *"Man shall not live on bread alone, but on every word that comes from the mouth of God"* (Matthew 4:4).

Scripture gives us a lineage of fasting rooted in deep communion:

Jesus fasted 40 days in the wilderness. Not to prove His worth, but to prepare His heart (Matthew 4:2). Moses fasted on Sinai, receiving the commandments that would shape a people (Exodus 34:28). The early church fasted before appointing leaders and making weighty decisions (Acts 13:2–3).

Each instance was less about food and more about focus. Less about hunger and more about holy dependence.

Fasting re-teaches us what sustains us. It untangles us from the grip of emotional eating, autopilot habits, and performative piety. It anchors us back into the truth: our bodies are not enemies to subdue or idols to worship. They are vessels through which we glorify God.

When you fast, you practice saying with your whole being:

"God, You are my portion. You are my sustainer. Not bread, not caffeine, not comfort food, You." And in that sacred hunger, you begin to feast. Not on food. But on presence.

Why Fasting Matters for Embodiment

Our culture is trained to numb discomfort at the first pang. We're conditioned to respond to every hunger whether its physical, emotional, spiritual with consumption. More food. More noise. More scrolling. But fasting is a holy interruption. It invites us to pause the pattern of immediate gratification and step into the sacred space of embodied surrender.

Fasting is not deprivation for deprivation's sake. It is a consecrated disruption. A chosen quieting of the flesh so we might listen more clearly to the Spirit. When we fast, we allow ourselves to feel hunger not to be mastered by it, but to meet God in it. We become reacquainted with our body's signals: the growl of the stomach, the ache of longing, the subtle awareness of need. But instead of medicating the moment, we meet it with Presence.

Scientific research on fasting affirms what Scripture has shown us for centuries: abstaining from food for a time can improve clarity, reset neural pathways, and even support cellular repair. But for the embodied believer, the deeper miracle isn't biological. It's spiritual alignment. Fasting invites your nervous system to shift from reactivity into regulation. It gives space for your parasympathetic system the part of our nervous system that tells us to rest and digest to settle, for your breath to deepen, and for your awareness to rise.

But above all, fasting brings the body back under the loving leadership of the Spirit. It reminds us: I am not ruled by appetite. I am not governed by cravings. I am led by Christ.

Jesus modeled this beautifully when He fasted for forty days in the wilderness before beginning His ministry (Matthew 4:2). In His hunger, He did not reach for provision apart from the Father. Instead, He declared, "Man shall not live by bread alone, but by every word that proceeds from the mouth of God" (Matthew 4:4). His fasting was not weakness it was preparation. Not punishment but power.

When you fast, you reclaim your body as a temple not of control, but of communion. You train yourself to listen, to yield, to be filled with something far more nourishing than calories: the very breath and Word of God.

In a world that numbs, fasting helps you feel again. In a world that runs, fasting helps you rest in surrender. It is one of the most countercultural and most embodied acts of worship we can offer.

Signs You're Practicing Spirit-Led Eating and Fasting

Spirit-led eating and fasting are not marked by rigidity, obsession, or shame. They are marked by reverence, presence, and trust. When you are led by the Spirit, both your plate and your practice reflect God's peace, not pressure. You begin to notice the sacred shift when.

You pause to pray before eating or fasting not out of guilt, but to invite God into the moment. You welcome the Spirit to guide your decision instead of defaulting to diet culture, emotional impulse, or legalism. This pause becomes holy ground.

You honor your body's God-designed cues. Hunger isn't feared or ignored; it's discerned. Fullness isn't resisted; it's respected. As research in interoceptive awareness shows, tuning into hunger and satiety strengthens emotional resilience and reduces disordered eating patterns (Herbert et al., 2013). But long before science confirmed it, Scripture already affirmed it: "Whether you eat or drink, do it all for the glory of God" (1 Corinthians 10:31).

You fast not to control outcomes but to connect. You're not trying to manipulate your body or twist God's hand. You're posturing your heart to be available, interruptible, and attuned to His whisper. You're letting go of comfort to make room for communion.

You feel the nearness of God in both hunger and fullness. Spirit-led living doesn't label one as more holy than the other. Instead, both become altars places where you meet the Lord in your body, whether empty or nourished. You sense that He is with you in every sensation, gently reminding you that you are not sustained by food alone.

You eat and fast from freedom, not fear. There is no striving to earn approval only abiding in grace. You no longer ask, "Am I doing this right?" but instead, "Is this drawing me closer to Jesus?" That shift changes everything. Because when you're rooted in His love, every bite and every fast becomes worship, not work.

Reflection Prompts
1. What messages about food, fasting, or hunger have shaped your habits?

2. Have I been using eating or fasting as a way to control or to connect?

3. How might fasting reconnect me to my body, mind, and spirit?

4. What fear about fasting do I need to surrender to God?

Embodied Prayer
Father,
You are the Bread of Life.
You are my Sustainer.
Forgive me for letting food or fear have more authority than You.
Teach me to eat with gratitude.
Teach me to fast with joy.
Teach me to listen to my body and lead it back to Your Spirit.
Make my hunger holy.
Make my satisfaction sacred.
Make my body Your dwelling place of peace.
In Jesus' name, Amen.

Covered & Held Stillness Practice
Hungering for God

Setup:
Sit or lie in a quiet place, hands resting lightly over your abdomen.

Practice:
Breathe deeply. Feel any hunger, fullness, or cravings rise without judgment.

Say aloud or silently:

> "I hunger for You more than anything else."

Let your body's sensations become an offering, not a shame. Let fasting and feasting both point you home.

Close with:

> "I am covered. I am held. I am nourished."

Movement-Based Exercise
Hunger Walk

Setup:
During a fast or meal transition, go for a slow, mindful walk.

Practice:

- Feel your body's sensations without needing to fix them.

- Pray with each step:

> "You sustain me. I trust You."

Finish by placing hands over your heart and stomach:

> "My hunger is holy. My body is home."

Chapter 15: Holy Rhythms of Nourishment

That each of them may eat and drink, and find satisfaction in all their toil—this is the gift of God.- Ecclesiastes 3:13

The Beloved Speaks

"I used to rush everything, my meals, workouts, even my prayers. Always hurrying toward a goal, a number, a 'new me.' But my body and spirit were exhausted. It wasn't until Coach De had me map out what it would look like to honor sacred rhythms: eating slower, resting deeper, moving more gently. That's when everything shifted. I found that real nourishment isn't just what you consume. It's how you live. And grace has its own rhythm." — The Beloved

We were never created for frantic living. Yet we often find ourselves trapped in the hurry that empties our bodies, burdens our minds, and starves our souls. From the very beginning, God orchestrated creation with intentional rhythms. Light and dark, day and night, planting and harvest, labor and rest (Genesis 1:14–18, Ecclesiastes 3:1–8). Each cycle an invitation, each rhythm divinely designed to anchor us in peace and replenish our strength.

Modern neuroscience underscores this ancient truth, revealing that our nervous systems thrive in patterns of regulated rhythm. When we abandon these rhythms, living in chronic hurry and stress, our sympathetic nervous system (our body's "fight or flight" response) remains activated. The result is a cascade of elevated cortisol, impaired digestion, increased anxiety, and emotional overwhelm. But when we slow down, when we align our pace with God's sacred tempo, the parasympathetic nervous system. The body's natural rest-and-digest response can soothe, restore, and heal us from within (Porges, 2011).

Nourishment was never intended to be frantic. It was always intended to be faithful. Our Creator crafted our bodies to digest food slowly, intentionally, prayerfully. Eating was never designed merely for survival or sustenance. It was created as communion, as gratitude embodied, as worshipful stewardship of the temple entrusted to us (1 Corinthians 6:19–20).

Faithful nourishment was foreign to me, not something taught, modeled, or even imagined. Growing up in a household of six children, every meal was a competitive sprint. The unspoken rule was clear: eat fast or eat less. Being the oldest, often feeling unseen or overlooked, I quickly learned that if I finished first, I secured the reward of second servings. Speed became synonymous with provision, recognition, and even love. Without realizing it, I was wiring my body, brain, and beliefs into patterns of scarcity and rush patterns that followed me into adulthood.

Today, I must consciously and continually choose to return to rhythm. It isn't automatic. It's a deliberate practice, cultivated through Spirit-led surrender. When I pause, slow down, and receive my food as a blessing rather than a battle, I step back into harmony with the sacred cadence God established at creation.

If you're resonating, here's how you can join me in this gentle journey toward faithful nourishment and embodied peace:

1. Pause and Breathe Before You Eat.
Take three slow breaths before every meal. Breathing deeply activates your vagus nerve, signaling your body that it is safe, reducing stress, and allowing your digestive system to fully engage.

2. Cultivate Gratitude.
Gratitude slows us down, reorients our focus, and shifts our neurobiology toward health. Begin meals by giving thanks, not just as a quick habit, but as a genuine acknowledgment of God's provision and care.

3. Engage Your Senses Intentionally.
Practice mindful eating by noticing textures, flavors, and aromas. Allow your senses to ground you in the present moment, shifting your eating from rushed necessity to restful nourishment.

4. Honor Your Body's Signals.
Tune into your hunger and fullness cues. Instead of racing to clear your plate, check in gently: Am I still hungry? Is my body satisfied? Listening deeply rebuilds trust between you and the temple God designed.

5. Release the Need for Speed.
Identify patterns or beliefs fueling hurried eating. Prayerfully ask God to reveal the root fear of lack, desire for control, or wounds from your past, and invite Him into healing. Practice slower bites, chew thoroughly, and savor each moment.

Faithful nourishment is not merely about the food we consume; it's about the posture with which we approach our meals. It's about reclaiming meals as holy spaces where our bodies, minds, and spirits are refreshed by God's presence and provision. When we reclaim these sacred rhythms, we don't merely heal our relationship with food. We heal our relationship with ourselves, with God, and with the holy cadence woven into creation itself.

God's Design for Rhythms of Nourishment

Rhythm is God's original language, spoken fluently through every anointed story since Eden. It is more than a mere pattern; it's His divine invitation to embodied trust and sustainable living. Scripture repeatedly invites us to live rhythmically, nourishingly, moment by moment, breath by breath. Grounded not in future anxieties but present grace.

Consider how God provided manna for His people in the wilderness (Exodus 16:4-5). Each morning, fresh sustenance fell gently from heaven enough, exactly enough, for that single day. There was no storing, no stockpiling, no saving for tomorrow. When the Israelites tried to hoard this divine provision, it spoiled. The message was clear: God's provision is not rooted in our anxious striving or frantic hoarding; it's grounded in daily, trusting dependence.

Neuroscience affirms this ancient wisdom: when we live anxiously, constantly striving to secure tomorrow, our bodies remain locked in chronic stress, elevating cortisol levels, impairing digestion, and weakening our immune system. Yet, when we trust daily living present in the assurance of divine sufficiency, our bodies shift into rhythms of calm, health, and restoration (Sapolsky, 2004).

Jesus embodied this rhythmic nourishment in His meals. From hillside picnics with thousands (John 6) to intimate breakfasts by the Sea of Galilee (John 21), He never rushed. Meals were not tasks to be checked off quickly; they were sacred spaces of communion, ministry, and healing. In His slow breaking of bread, Jesus modeled the deep neurological truth that our bodies digest and absorb nourishment best when we eat calmly and relationally. Shared meals activate our parasympathetic nervous system. Our body's "rest-and-digest" state encourages deeper connection, better digestion, and emotional regulation (Siegel, 2012). Jesus knew this intuitively, setting a divine precedent: eating is worshipful, restorative, and inherently communal.

But Jesus didn't just model slow nourishment. He commanded restful rhythms explicitly. After intense periods of ministry, He gently invited His disciples, *"Come away by yourselves to a desolate place and rest a while"* (Mark 6:31). The Son of God Himself observed intentional patterns of rest and renewal, teaching us that work without restorative rhythms leads not to fruitfulness but burnout. Modern research confirms that deliberate rest is essential for physical health, emotional resilience, and spiritual vitality. Rest replenishes neurotransmitters, repairs neural pathways, and resets our nervous systems, enabling clearer thinking, healthier bodies, and more vibrant spirits (Walker, 2017).

To live nourished is, at its deepest core, an expression of trust, not in the relentless demands of this hurried world, but in the unwavering faithfulness of our God who always provides. This trust is beautifully encapsulated in Jesus' prayer, *"Give us today our daily bread"* (Matthew 6:11, NIV). It's an embodied prayer, a surrendering prayer. A prayer that gently leads us out of anxiety into daily dependence, out of hustle into holy rhythms.

How can you practically cultivate these rhythms in your daily life as the Embodied Beloved?

1. Begin Your Day with "Daily Manna" Moments
Each morning, spend a quiet moment of intentional stillness. Breathe deeply, placing your hand over your heart and reciting slowly, "Lord, give me today's bread, today's peace, today's portion." Let your nervous system settle into this divine assurance.

2. Embrace Slow, Intentional Meals
Practice eating without rush or distraction. Create spaces, even briefly, where meals become acts of worship and communion. Chew slowly, savor each bite, and let gratitude rise within you. Share meals regularly in the community, mirroring Jesus' model of nourishment as ministry.

3. Schedule Sacred Rest
Intentionally designate times for rest. Whether it's weekly Sabbath observance, daily quiet moments, or seasonal retreats, honor your body's need for restorative rhythms. Rest is not indulgent; it is sacred obedience. Your body will respond with healing and renewed strength.

4. Reflect Daily on God's Faithfulness
Each evening, pause to recount moments of provision throughout your day. This simple reflection rewires your brain toward trust and gratitude, strengthening neural pathways associated with peace, reducing stress, and enhancing emotional resilience.

As you align your days with these holy rhythms, you step fully into what it means to be the Embodied Beloved: living nourished, deeply rooted in trust, harmonizing body, soul, and spirit with the timeless rhythm of God's sustaining grace.

Selah Moment: Breath Prayer
Inhale: You provide my daily bread.
Exhale: I rest in Your rhythm.
Let this breath prayer slow your body, center your mind, and anchor you in God's sufficiency.

Why Rhythm Matters for Your Body

The body thrives in rhythmic patterns.Circadian rhythms govern our sleep-wake cycles, hormone release, digestion, and metabolism. Studies show that consistent patterns of eating and resting improve insulin sensitivity, reduce inflammation, and optimize metabolic health (Sutton et al., 2018).

Conversely, erratic eating patterns, chronic rushing, and stress-induced digestion disruption activate the sympathetic "fight or flight" system. Over time, this leads to elevated cortisol, impaired immunity, and gut dysregulation (Sapolsky, 2004). Your body was designed to anticipate nourishment, not as a reaction to fear, but as a relational rhythm with God and yourself.

The nervous system, too, is calibrated for predictable cycles of nourishment and rest. Trauma, chronic stress, and hustle culture fracture these cycles. Healing often begins by re-establishing gentle, predictable rhythms that signal safety and trust.

To eat with rhythm is not simply a nutritional practice. It is an act of worship, aligning body, mind, and spirit with the tempo of divine grace.

You eat in response to true hunger and fullness, not emotional urgency or external pressure. When you're living nourished, your eating begins to flow from attunement rather than anxiety. You notice when your body whispers hunger, not just when it screams. You trust that fullness is a cue for peace, not punishment. Instead of eating in reaction to stress, shame, or social norms, you eat from a grounded place of internal wisdom. What science calls interoceptive awareness. The Holy Spirit, dwelling within you, heightens this awareness, allowing you to honor your body's signals without fear or guilt (Romans 8:11). You become more Spirit-led than schedule-driven, more anchored than reactive.

1.You rest before exhaustion demands collapse.
In holy rhythms, rest is no longer a last resort. It becomes a faithful, proactive rhythm, not performative. You don't wait for your body to scream for a break. You anticipate your need for restoration and respond with gentleness. Like Jesus, who regularly withdrew to quiet places (Luke 5:16), you honor the reality that your worth is not measured by how much you produce, but by your willingness to abide. Biologically, this rhythm strengthens your parasympathetic nervous system, reducing inflammation, boosting immunity, and renewing your capacity for resilience.

2.You seek "daily bread" living, releasing the temptation to stockpile or control. You no longer live in survival mode, hoarding food, time, or energy "just in case." Instead, you live in the posture of Exodus 16. Trusting that God's manna will meet you every morning. You release the illusion of control and surrender to the sufficiency of Christ. This doesn't mean you stop planning or stewarding well. It means you no longer grip life with clenched fists. Your nourishment flows from trust, not panic. Your peace becomes physiological, not just spiritual. Cortisol levels drop. Breath deepens. The body stops bracing. You are held.

3. You savor meals as moments of gratitude, not guilt.
You bless the food before you, not curse yourself for needing it. You let go of the cultural scripts that demonize eating and instead reclaim meals as an act of worship. Like Jesus breaking bread and giving thanks (Luke 22:19), you make your table a holy place. Gratitude activates your brain's reward pathways in a healthy way, releasing dopamine not from indulgence or restriction, but from joy. This sacred pause allows your nervous system to soften, your digestion to work as designed, and your heart to return to rest.

4. You experience satisfaction, not merely of the stomach, but of the spirit. In holy rhythms, fullness becomes more than a physical cue. It becomes a spiritual alignment. You feel nourished in ways that go beyond calories or macros. Your meals, your rest, your days begin to align with the Father's voice and cadence. There is a deep soul-satisfaction that reminds you: *I am fed, I am filled, I am free.* You eat and move and breathe not as someone trying to earn love, but as someone who already has it.

To live nourished is to dwell near the heartbeat of God, present, provided for, and at peace. This is the rhythm of the Embodied Beloved: no longer ruled by appetite or anxiety, but rooted in trust, gratitude, and grace.

From Frenzied Feasting to Sacred Nourishment

Without rhythm, even the good and beautiful things, food, movement, and ministry, become burdens instead of blessings. We find ourselves overwhelmed, caught in cycles of striving that leave us depleted rather than filled. God didn't design nourishment to be yet another space of anxious effort. He created it to be a sanctuary, a space of replenishment and renewal.

Research echoes this sacred design, showing that when our lives lack healthy, consistent rhythms, our bodies and brains struggle. Chronic hurry and unregulated eating patterns trigger persistent stress responses, flooding our system with cortisol, the hormone that signals alarm. In this heightened state, digestion falters, immunity weakens, emotional resilience diminishes, and our spirits grow weary (Sapolsky, 2004). The frantic pace we keep rushing through meals, multitasking during ministry, and racing from one demand to the next directly contradicts the gentle tempo God set into motion at creation.

Frantic feeding whispers urgent lies into our hearts: "You must hurry. You must hustle. You're falling behind." But holy rhythms speak truth and invite us tenderly into rest: "Pause. Receive. You are already seen, known, and held." This is the profound difference between living according to the world's demands and receiving life according to the Spirit's invitation.

In Scripture, we see this rhythm modeled by Jesus Himself, who regularly withdrew to quiet places, stepping away from crowds and busyness (Mark 1:35, Luke 5:16). Jesus never lived frantically. He lived intentionally. He showed us how to pause amid chaos, how to listen deeply, how to find sustenance not just in bread alone but in every word from the Father (Matthew 4:4).

When nourishment is driven by the hurried heart, food becomes another battleground of achievement and scarcity, another place where we try, and inevitably fail to fill ourselves. But when nourishment is anchored in rhythm, meals transform into a holy pause, spaces of surrender, gratitude, and embodied worship.

To shift from frantic striving into holy rhythm, I invite you into these gentle practices:

1. Begin with Stillness.
Before reaching for your plate, pause. Allow yourself a moment of stillness, taking several slow breaths. Invite the Spirit's peace into your body, calming the hurried heart.

2. Embrace Gratitude as Worship.
Offer simple gratitude, acknowledging provision as an expression of God's kindness. Gratitude shifts the brain's patterns away from scarcity and anxiety toward joy, generosity, and fullness.

3. Receive Rather than Rush.
Eat slowly and intentionally. As you savor each bite, remind yourself: "I am already held. I am already cared for. I am already enough." Allow this truth to transform your meal from frantic feeding to faithful receiving.

4. Honor Your Body's Sacred Cues.
Pay gentle attention to hunger and fullness. God created these signals as gifts, guiding you toward balance and

self-care. Trusting these bodily cues rebuilds your capacity to listen and respond with kindness rather than control.

5. Cultivate Rhythms of Grace in Daily Life.
Extend rhythm beyond your meals into movement, ministry, and rest. Create margin in your day. Honor your body's needs for sleep, stillness, and joyful movement. These holy rhythms realign your life with the Spirit's pace rather than the world's frantic urgency.

Beloved, you were never meant to live endlessly striving. You were created to dwell securely in rhythms of grace. The world may always shout for more; more productivity, more speed, more striving, but the Spirit gently whispers, "Receive what is sufficient. You are enough."

Practices to Reclaim Holy Nourishment
Practice Daily Bread Living
Release the anxiety of future stockpiling. Ask yourself each morning, "What does my body, my mind, and my spirit need today?" Trust God for provision one day at a time.

Slow Your Eating
Put your fork down between bites. Breathe. Offer a whispered prayer of gratitude. Let eating become a spiritual practice of presence rather than a task of performance.

Rest Before You Collapse
Do not wait for burnout to remind you that you are human. Build sacred pauses into your week, treating them as appointments with your Creator.

Sabbath Your Soul
Once a week, create a meal experience that is unrushed,

joyful, and fully present. Invite laughter. Invite gratitude. Invite stillness. Let it be an altar of delight before the Lord.

> *"He makes me lie down in green pastures, he leads me beside quiet waters, he refreshes my soul."* — Psalm 23:2-3 (NIV)

Reflection Prompts

1. How has rushing shaped the way you eat, move, and live?

2. Where is God inviting you to slow down and savor more?

3. What would it look like to nourish your body and your spirit with rhythms of grace rather than striving?

4. How can you embody "daily bread living" in your fitness, food, and rest this week?

Embodied Prayer

Father,
Thank You for designing my body, my life, and my days with rhythms of flourishing.
Forgive me for rushing through what You meant for me to savor.
Forgive me for measuring my worth by my productivity rather than by Your presence.
Teach me to move, to eat, to work, and to rest in Your pace, not mine.
Give me grace to live in daily dependence, not frantic striving.
Let true nourishment flood every part of me body, mind, and soul.
In Jesus' name, Amen.

Covered & Held Stillness Practice
Breath Between Bites

Setup:
Prepare a small, nourishing snack or meal. Create a quiet environment without screens or distractions.

Practice:
Before eating, pause and pray aloud:
"Lord, thank You for this provision."

Take a bite.
Put your utensil down.
Breathe deeply three times before picking it up again.
Let each breath be a reminder:
"I am not in a race. I am in a relationship."

Close your meal with the prayer:
"I have tasted and seen that You are good."

Movement-Based Exercise
Rhythmic Gratitude Walk

Setup:
After a meal or restful moment, take a slow 5–10 minute walk outdoors.

Practice:
With each step, breathe a prayer of gratitude:
"Thank You for today's bread."
"Thank You for this body that moves."
"Thank You for teaching me to slow down."

Let your breathing and walking become a form of embodied worship.

Ready to put what you've read into practice?
Download the FaithFueled Life App and take your journey deeper. Inside, you'll find guided breath prayers, embodied movement sessions, Scripture meditations, and soul-strengthening practices that bring this book to life. Whether you're seeking stillness, strength, or spiritual renewal, the app gives you real-time tools to embody your faith and steward your temple; anytime, anywhere.

Don't just read about transformation. Live it.
www.tinyurl.com/FAITHFUELEDAPP and begin your journey of becoming the Embodied Beloved.

Chapter 16: What Do I Eat? How Much? Why?

Then God said, 'I give you every seed-bearing plant on the face of the whole earth and every tree that has fruit with seed in it. They will be yours for food.' —Genesis 1:29 (NIV)

The Beloved Speaks
"I've spent years chasing every diet plan out there counting calories, mimicking someone else's routine. Yet something always felt off. Then I began uncovering God's design for nourishment, and everything shifted. This isn't about rigid rules or performance. It's about finding a rhythm aligned with His goodness. It's not wrapped in fear; it's rooted in freedom. I came to Coach De looking for a plan and she redirected me. I had simply forgotten what it was like to eat with trust and simplicity. Today, I'm learning to come back to eat with joy, gratitude, and complete freedom in His provision."-The Beloved

God's Nourishment Is Simple, Not Stressful
God was the first and final authority on nourishment. Long before nutrition labels, calorie counts, or food pyramids, there was Eden lush, abundant, and enough. In the garden, nourishment wasn't calculated or earned. It was simply *given*. There was no striving, no shame, no scarcity; only provision. God, in His goodness, placed humanity in a setting where food wasn't just functional. It was sacred. It was beauty. It was communion.

But then came the twist in the story. The enemy didn't attack Eve's body. He went after her trust. And he did it through food. That first act of disobedience wasn't just a bite. It was a breach. A rupture in rhythm. A severing from the simplicity and sufficiency of God's provision. What God had called "good," the serpent clouded with doubt:

"Did God really say?" (Genesis 3:1).

And ever since, food has carried more than nutrients. It's carried shame, confusion, and fear. We see the ripple of that brokenness in our own lives today. Nutrition, once a natural rhythm, has become a war zone for many women. We vacillate between control and chaos. Strict plans that punish our bodies and unbridled indulgence that disconnects us from them. We idolize discipline, demonize hunger, and spiritualize restriction, calling it "clean" or "obedient," when often it's just another mask for fear. The enemy still whispers the same lie: *"God is holding out on you."*

But Beloved, God's design hasn't changed. He is still the Provider. His invitation is still one of peace, not punishment. We don't need another diet or food rule. We need redemption. We need to return; not to a food plan, but to the One who designed our bodies and our nourishment in perfect harmony.

When we *re-member* when we come back to our bodies as temples and our meals as moments of worship. We find what was never lost in Him: simplicity, satisfaction, and holy connection. Food becomes more than fuel. It becomes an altar. A place where the physical and the spiritual intertwine. A daily reminder that He is near. That He is enough. And that His provision is always personal, purposeful, and good.

Selah Moment: Breath Prayer

Inhale: You provide, Lord.
Exhale: I receive with gratitude.

Inhale: You nourish every part of me.
Exhale: I release shame and confusion.

Inhale: My body is your temple.
Exhale: I choose peace, not punishment.

What Do I Eat? How Much? Why?

The better question isn't "What should I eat?" it's How does God invite me to be nourished? Because nourishment is not just a set of rules to follow or numbers to track. It's a relationship to restore. From the beginning, God wove nourishment into the very fabric of our existence. His provision was whole, beautiful, abundant, and simple. But over time, we've drifted. We've allowed culture to overcomplicate what God made clear. We've traded divine rhythms for worldly restrictions and lost the ability to hear the Spirit through the body.

In a world of rigid formulas and fear-based eating, the invitation is not to tighten our grip, but to return to the garden, to the Giver, to our God-designed wisdom. This is not about compliance. It's about communion. We align our nourishment not by adopting the latest trend, but by attuning to the voice of the Creator who handcrafted our bodies with precision and love. The same God who knit your digestive, hormonal, and nervous systems together also gave you hunger cues, cravings, and cycles that mirror His seasons and grace.

So instead of asking, What do I have to eat? We ask, "How can I eat in a way that honors what God has created, both on my plate and within me?" We eat to worship, not to war. We eat to remember who we are and whose we are. We eat to be equipped for every good work He's called us to do. And as we learn to listen, deeply, humbly, and gently. We begin to receive food not with anxiety, but with awe.

What Do I Eat?

I teach from a simple principle: God's food still works. Whole, God-made nourishment; fruits, vegetables, grains, legumes, seeds, clean water, lean meats, and healthy fats was designed not only to sustain us but to support the intricate systems of our bodies: hormones, digestion, immunity, cognition, energy, and emotional regulation. It's not complicated. I call it F.O.O.D.

Fresh Fruits and Vegetables as close to its original state as possible.

Omega 3s and 6s found in legumes, nuts and fish.

Organic (or natural, kosher) proteins- plant or animal you choose but both are a good idea.

Drink water (no substitutes and not sparkling)

You've heard it before. The human body thrives on what the earth produces. When we eat in alignment with creation, we partner with the healing design of our Creator.

But just as important as *what* we eat is *how* we receive it. I don't teach restriction. I teach rhythm. Eating isn't meant to be reactionary or shame-driven. Instead, we create rhythms that support our energy, regulate our nervous system, and invite peace. Balanced meals built on protein, fiber-rich carbohydrates, and healthy fats help stabilize blood sugar, reduce inflammation, and support hormone health. But they also do something more sacred. They help us become present. Attuned. Aware of God's provision in the moment.

No food group is inherently evil. No macronutrient is a moral issue. Variety is a form of grace. It teaches us to receive freely, joyfully, and with discernment.

From the beginning, God wove nourishment into the structure of creation itself. And each day of creation reveals a principle we can align with in how we eat, move, and live.

The Creation Framework of Nourishment:
Day 1: Light and Dark
Our circadian rhythms matter. Vitamin D regulates serotonin and mood. Melatonin, produced in darkness, restores us. Your digestion and metabolism work best in alignment with light. Eat during the day. Rest at night. Respect your rhythms.

Day 2: Land and Sea
Earth and ocean provide what your body needs. Grains, vegetables, and legumes from the land. Omega-3s and minerals from fish and sea plants. Both were created to nourish and sustain life.

Day 3: Seed-Bearing Plants
God said these were *"for food."* Whole grains, legumes, seeds, leafy greens. These foods regulate blood sugar, reduce inflammation, and heal the gut. Diversity in plants builds resilience in the body.

Day 4: Sun and Moon
You were designed for rhythm. When we eat out of sync with our design late-night snacking, stress-driven grazing. We disrupt not just digestion, but the nervous system and hormones. Return to rest. Return to light.

Day 5: Birds and Fish (Lean Proteins)
Lean protein from clean sources repairs muscle, balances hormones, and sustains energy. It's not about macro obsession. It's about honoring what your body needs.

Day 6: Animals and Humans
Stewardship matters. Ethical, sustainable, God-honoring choices, whether meat, dairy, or eggs. Allow us to eat with peace. You are not what you eat. But your choices reflect what you value.

Day 7: Rest and Recovery
Sabbath isn't just spiritual. It's physiological. Rest slows the nervous system, improves digestion, and supports repair. Mindful eating is Sabbath for the gut. Let your food settle. Let your soul exhale.

How Much?
There is no "one-size-fits-all" portion. Why? Because you are not static. WIth my clients I can't give them a single answer because the human body is dynamic, seasonal, and consecrated. How much we eat should honor not just our

hunger but our healing. Some seasons require more. Others invite stillness and recalibration. The key is to stay connected to your inner signals. Your God-given hunger and fullness cues. These are the Spirit's whispers within the body, telling you when you need nourishment and when you've received enough. For many of us, recognizing our body's signals has become difficult. Sometimes even impossible, because over the years, we've learned to disconnect, numb, or override them. The natural hunger cues that were designed to tell us when we're hungry or full have been silenced or ignored.

We are not meant to override those signals with external rules, labels, or apps. Science confirms what Scripture and the Spirit already teach: intuitive eating. The ability to honor internal hunger and satiety. Leads to more stable metabolism, better mental health, and increased body trust (Tylka & Kroon Van Diest, 2013). It's not "letting yourself go". It's learning to be guided by the Holy Spirit, not by shame or performance.

Portion sizes should serve your purpose, whether you are rebuilding strength, balancing hormones, recovering from stress, or maintaining wellness. This is *stewardship*, not perfection. Structured freedom will always take you farther than rigid fear. I have been the woman who weighed every gram and counted every macro and I am here to say. You can not live life on a diet. Many do but its a tether to the scale and it takes space in your life that can be enjoyed elsewhere.

There is no "one-size-fits-all" portion. Why? Because you are not static. You are seasonal, sacred, and shifting. Some days you're rebuilding. Others, recovering. Some seasons require more. Others, less.

So how much should you eat? Enough to honor your hunger not numb your emotions. Enough to sustain not strain. You were not designed to be micromanaged by apps or trackers. You were designed to be led by the Spirit even in your eating.

Intuitive eating, supported by Scripture and science alike, cultivates better blood sugar regulation, stronger metabolic flexibility, and more body trust (Tylka & Kroon Van Diest, 2013). Hunger and fullness cues are not to be feared. They are to be *formed* and *followed*.

What your body needs today may differ from what it needed last year or what it will need tomorrow. That's why I don't teach rigid portion control. I teach Spirit-led stewardship.

How much you eat should honor not just your hunger, but your healing. Some seasons require more fuel. Rebuilding strength, balancing hormones, walking through stress. Other seasons may invite stillness, restoration, or recalibration. The key is learning to listen to your internal cues. Your God-given hunger and fullness signals. These are the Spirit's whispers through the body, gently saying, *"enough,"* or *"you need more."*

But I also believe in offering *grace-filled structure*. One practical tool I teach is the a hand-based portion control method developed by nutrition scientists, designed to offer personalized guidance using your own hand size as a proportional tool.

It's simple, flexible, and here's the most powerful part. It's based on the body God gave *you.* No food scale required. No tracking app needed. Just the unique anatomy of your hand, fearfully and wonderfully made (Psalm 139:14).

Because your hand is proportionate to your body, it serves as a built-in measuring tool that adjusts to your personal size, metabolism, and needs:

- Palm = Protein
  One palm-sized portion per meal for women (two for men) is a great place to start. This is your lean meats, fish, eggs, tofu, etc.

- Fist = Vegetables
  Fill at least one fist-sized portion (or more!) of colorful, non-starchy vegetables.

- Cupped Hand = Carbohydrates
  Think of fruits, grains, legumes, or starchy veggies like sweet potatoes. One cupped hand portion for women (two for men).

- Thumb = Healthy Fats
  Avocados, nuts, seeds, oils. One thumb-sized portion per meal.

This isn't a formula. It's a framework. It teaches you to approach your plate with intention, not obsession. It removes the fear and returns you to wisdom. And it reminds you that the tools God placed in your body. Your hands, your cues, your breath, are not broken. They are blessed.

So instead of asking, *"Is this the right amount?"* try asking, *"Is this amount serving my season?"* Because *stewardship* adapts. And it always starts with awareness, not anxiety.

Why?

Because *you are the temple* (1 Corinthians 6:19). You are the dwelling place of God's Spirit. That means how you care for your body isn't vanity. It's *veneration*.

Because nourishment is an act of worship. When we eat with gratitude and give thanks to the One who provides (Deuteronomy 8:10).Every bite can become a form of gratitude. Every meal, a table where we receive what God freely gives.

Because food was *never* the curse. It was part of the blessing given in Eden, reaffirmed by Jesus who broke bread, and sanctified through thanksgiving. The curse was confusion and control. God's design is always clarity and peace.

And because what we eat impacts *everything*. From our gut to our brain to our hormones and mood, nourishment plays a powerful role in emotional regulation, cognitive clarity, sleep quality, and energy for our Kingdom purpose. When we nourish well, we're not just feeding the body. We're strengthening the vessel through which God moves.

Reflection Prompts

1. What messages about food did I learn growing up? How do they shape my habits today?

2. Do I eat from a place of celebration or control?

3. Where have I allowed fear or guilt to replace grace in my eating patterns?

4. What would it look like to receive food as worship instead of warfare?

Embodied Prayer

Father,
You are the Bread of Life and the Living Water.
You've never withheld what I need.
Teach me to return to Your rhythms of nourishment simple, holy, and good.
Strip away the confusion. Silence the voice of shame.
Let every bite be a moment of communion,
Every meal a table of grace,
And every craving an invitation to come back to You.
I receive your provision, Lord,
Not with fear, but with faith.
Amen.

Covered & Held Stillness Practice: "Open Hands, Open Heart"

Position: Sit upright in a chair or on the floor. Place your hands open, palms up on your lap.

Breath: Inhale deeply through the nose for 4 counts, exhale through the mouth for 6.

Visualization: Imagine God's provision resting gently in your open palms, food, peace, love.

Mantra: "God is not a God of confusion. He nourishes me with clarity and grace."
Duration: 3–5 minutes.

Movement-Based Practice: "Grace-Filled Nourishment Flow"

Warm-Up: Gentle neck rolls, shoulder shrugs, and hip circles.
Movement:

March in place while saying aloud: "Thank you, Lord, for my body."

Inhale arms overhead, exhale into a forward fold; repeat 3x.

Gentle side lunges to stretch the inner thighs; left, then right; repeat 10x each.

Bring hands to heart, bow head in gratitude.

Cool Down:

Sit or lie down. Rub your belly gently, blessing your digestive system.

Whisper: "This is my temple. I nourish it in love."

Part 5: Whole Life Integration

Rooted. Radiant. Whole.

You were never meant to live fragmented.
Transformation is not confined to fitness, food, or mindset alone it spills into every corner of life.

This final part is where your healing becomes your new way of living: rooted in Christ, radiant with grace, bearing lasting fruit in every area of your life.

Chapter 17: Holy Habits, Not Hustle Routines

"Have nothing to do with godless myths and old wives' tales; rather, train yourself to be godly. For physical training is of some value, but godliness has value for all things, holding promise for both the present life and the life to come."
- 1 Timothy 4:7–8

The Beloved Speaks

"I used to think routines were the answer. That if I could just find the perfect morning routine, the right plan, the best tracker. I'd finally feel at peace. But no matter how hard I tried, it never stuck. I kept burning out. What I needed wasn't more structure. I needed to surrender. When I started building habits with God instead of for Him, everything changed. Now I have rhythms, not rules. Presence, not pressure. My habits are holy now, not heavy." — The Beloved

The world preaches hustle like it's holy. It promises that if you just wake up earlier, grind harder, and self-optimize better, you'll finally arrive at a life that matters. But here's the truth: hustle is a counterfeit gospel. It feeds the illusion that your worth is earned through effort, and your rest must be deserved.

But the Kingdom of God tells a radically different story. One not built on burnout, but on belovedness. In God's economy, fruitfulness flows from faithfulness not frantic striving. Jesus said it plainly: "Remain in me, as I also remain in you. No branch can bear fruit by itself; it must remain in the vine"

(John 15:4, NIV). We were never called to strain harder. We were always called to stay closer.

Abiding isn't passive. It's powerful. It's not laziness, it's trust. It's not inaction. It's an intimate dependence. And for me, it was a game-changer. I'll never forget the moment: during an experiential prayer session, we were invited to write the lies the enemy had looped in our minds on a balloon. Then we popped the balloon literally taking those lies captive. My balloon revealed one simple, sacred word: ABIDE. The tears came quickly, not just from emotion but from freedom. In that moment, the Spirit whispered something I've never forgotten: "The enemy drives, but the Father invites."

That was the turning point. I stopped hustling for God and started walking with Him. I stopped proving and started receiving. My entire heart posture shifted from urgency to intimacy, from anxiety to trust. And as neuroscience confirms, this shift matters. When we live from a place of secure attachment spiritually, emotionally, and physically our nervous systems begin to regulate. Our minds heal. Our choices align. We become whole.

You were never created to grip life in survival mode. You were meant to abide. And when you do, you discover this sacred truth: you don't have to hustle for a seat at the table. You already belong.

Why Hustle Fails (Even When It "Works")

Hustle might get you quick results. It might land you the promotion, the progress photo, or the praise. But it can't heal what's aching beneath the surface. It can't nourish a weary soul. And let's be honest. What's the point of reaching your goals if you're too exhausted, anxious, or disconnected to enjoy them?

Hustle trains the body to perform but starves the heart of presence. You can lose weight and still despise your reflection. You can gain followers and still feel invisible. You can plan every hour of your day and still miss the peace that passes understanding. That's because routines without revelation will always run dry. Busyness without embodiment becomes bondage.

True transformation doesn't come from doing more. It comes from abiding more deeply.

Jesus said, "I am the vine; you are the branches. If you remain in me and I in you, you will bear much fruit; apart from me you can do nothing" (John 15:5, NIV). Fruitfulness is the overflow of connectedness not the outcome of control.

Science affirms what Scripture has long declared. Chronic overwork and stress elevate cortisol, weaken the immune system, increase inflammation, and impair emotional regulation (McEwen, 2007). Our bodies were not built to carry constant pressure. But when we anchor ourselves in rhythms of rest, prayer, breath, and embodied gratitude, the parasympathetic nervous system activates bringing calm, clarity, and healing (Porges, 2011).

Your body, like your soul, was designed for sustainable rhythms not survival mode. In God's design, presence always precedes productivity. And abiding? That's where the real transformation begins.

My Story: Breaking Up with Busyness

For years, I believed hustle was holy. I wore busyness like a badge of honor. I thought if I could just accomplish more, serve harder, wake up earlier, do it all "for God," I would finally feel at peace.

But the more I hustled, the emptier I became.

I confused being productive with being purposeful. I thought a packed schedule equaled a full life. But somewhere along the way, the girl who loved Jesus started running too fast to even hear His voice.

God, in His mercy, brought me to a breaking point. Not because He was punishing me, but because He loved me too much to let me keep running on fumes.

I realized that busyness wasn't making me more fruitful.
It was making me more fragile.
It wasn't strengthening my soul.
It was starving it.

One day, as I sat overwhelmed in my car after yet another overcommitted day, the Holy Spirit gently whispered a truth I'll never forget:

"I never asked you to be busy. I asked you to be with Me."

It wrecked me. In the best way.

That was the beginning of my breakup with hustle. It didn't happen overnight. I still catch myself sometimes reaching for busyness like a safety blanket. But now, by grace, I recognize the warning signs:

The shallow breathing.
The short temper.
The nagging pressure to "do more" to "be enough."

Now, I choose a different rhythm. I choose presence over performance.
Abiding over arriving.
Rhythms of grace over routines of guilt.

And you can too.

Pause and Reflect: Are You Carrying a Yoke Jesus Never Gave You?

Take a breath.

Before you keep reading, I want you to pause.

Close your eyes for a moment and ask yourself:

- Where am I hustling for approval that's already been given?

- What expectations am I carrying that God never asked me to hold?

- Have I confused faithfulness with busyness?

- Am I building routines that nourish my soul or numb it?

Beloved, Jesus doesn't hand out burnout.
He doesn't drive us into exhaustion.
He invites us into rest.

"Truly my soul finds rest in God; my salvation comes from him. Yes, my soul, find rest in God; my hope comes from him."
Psalm 62:1,5

You don't have to earn your way into peace.
You can lay it all down right here, and walk in grace instead.

What Makes a Habit Holy?
Not every habit that helps us is holy, but every holy habit helps us become who we were created to be. A holy habit is more than a routine or discipline. It is a sacred rhythm that aligns your lived actions with your identity as the Beloved of God. These habits don't flow from performance or perfectionism; they flow from your position in Christ fully known, fully loved, fully held.

Holy habits are sustainable because they are built on grace, not guilt. They bend with the seasons of your life instead of breaking you beneath the weight of "shoulds."

Neuroscience reminds us that our brains are shaped by what we practice (Hebb, 1949). The more we move, think, and live from a place of rest in God's love, the more those neural pathways of peace and trust deepen. Holy habits renew the mind and restore the nervous system. They create space in the body for the Spirit to dwell richly.

These habits aren't about earning God's favor you already have that. They are about embodying the truth of your Belovedness in everyday choices. They are not ladders to climb but pathways to abide.

Examples of Holy Habits:

- Moving your body as an act of reverence, because it is a temple not a project to fix.
- Eating slowly, savoring your food with gratitude instead of guilt, remembering that nourishment is a form of worship.
- Praying while walking, letting your body carry your heart to God instead of letting anxiety drive your scrolling.
- Planning your week around peace instead of productivity, anchoring your rhythms in presence rather than pressure.
- Honoring Sabbath as a radical act of trust in God's provision, not a weakness to overcome.

These practices are not legalistic demands. They are invitations into deeper intimacy. They are sacred, Spirit-led rhythms that help you live rooted in the truth: You are the Beloved. You are already enough. And now, in grace, you're learning to live like it.

The Pattern of Jesus

Jesus did not hurry through life. He moved with intention, rooted in communion with the Father. His life revealed what holy embodiment looks like in human form fully divine, fully human, fully present. His habits were not performative; they were relational. Sacred. Sustainable. A rhythm of grace, not grind.

Scripture shows us His holy patterns:

He rose early not for productivity, but for presence. "Very early in the morning, while it was still dark, Jesus got up... and prayed" (Mark 1:35).

He often withdrew to lonely places not to escape people, but to embrace intimacy with the Father (Luke 5:16).

He fasted not to punish His body, but to align His appetite with the will of God.

He feasted not with guilt, but with purpose, sharing table fellowship that restored dignity to the outcast and joy to the weary.

And when His body was tired, He honored its need for rest even when the demands around Him were urgent (Mark 6:31).

Jesus, the Son of God, was not driven by grind culture. He wasn't hustling for healing or rushing through His ministry checklist. He modeled something far more countercultural: grace culture. A life attuned to the Father's voice, not the world's volume.

He lived in the "unforced rhythms of grace" (Matthew 11:29, MSG) a holy cadence that invites us to unlearn our frantic striving and relearn His faithful, embodied pace.

Jesus' way wasn't rushed. It was rooted. Not frantic, but faithful. And as His Beloved, we are invited to learn from Him not just in belief, but in embodied practice. His pace is the one our nervous systems long for, our souls crave, and our bodies were made to follow.

Selah Moment: Breath Prayer

Inhale: I abide in Your grace.
Exhale: I release the need to strive.

Creating Your Own Holy Rhythms

Freedom doesn't come from rigid discipline. It's formed in rhythms where grace makes room for your humanity. Cultivated in the quiet, surrendered spaces where God meets you.

It flows from Spirit-led rhythms yoked to grace habits that align your body, mind, and spirit with the presence of God.

1. Start small. Start sacred.

- Transformation is not a sprint; it's a slow turning of the soul toward what is true. Begin with one holy habit that roots you in presence:
- A five-minute morning check-in with God before the world gets your attention, give it to the One who holds your breath.
- Drinking water before coffee not as a wellness trend, but as a quiet act of reverence for the temple you live in.
- Reading one verse of Scripture before reaching for your phone letting the Word shape your day before the world does.

These micro-practices carry macro-impact. Neuroscience calls this "habit stacking" anchoring a new behavior to an existing routine to increase consistency (Clear, 2018). But we call it worship offering even the smallest rhythms to God.

2. Anchor your habits to what matters.

- Tie movement to worship: walk and pray. Let your breath bear intercession. Let your body echo devotion.
- Link meals to gratitude: pause to breathe, bless, and behold the gift of nourishment.
- End your day not with replayed regrets, but with reflection. Let the Spirit gently reveal, renew, and restore.

Adapt, don't abandon. Life will shift. Schedules will stretch. Seasons will surprise you. Let your rhythms flex with grace instead of breaking under shame.

Grace doesn't quit it pivots. Celebrate consistency, not perfection. Perfection is not the goal being filled with God's presence is.

Progress slow, stuttering, set apart is still holy. You're not failing when you show up imperfectly. You're embodying faithfulness. And that pleases the heart of God.

In God's economy, small is sacred. In His kingdom, showing up again and again especially when it's hard is what bears fruit. Faithfulness is fruitfulness.

Reflection Prompts

1. What habits in your life feel life-giving? Which feel heavy?

2. Where have you let hustle sneak in under the name of discipline?

3. What is one habit you'd like to make holy this week?

4. How can you invite Jesus into your daily rhythms more intentionally?

Embodied Prayer

Jesus,
I release my addiction to hustle and performance.
I no longer want habits fueled by fear and striving.
I want rhythms that root me in You.
Teach me to walk in the unforced rhythms of Your grace.
Let my routines reflect my reliance, not my resentment.
Show me that small steps in Your presence are greater than grand strides without You.
Help me trust that growth comes not from grinding harder, but from abiding deeper.
Thank You for inviting me to live whole, free, and nourished in You.
In Your name, Amen.

Covered & Held Stillness Practice: Rooted Rhythms

Setup:
Find a quiet place to sit or lie down. Place one hand on your heart and one hand on your stomach.

Practice:
Breathe slowly. Imagine yourself like a tree planted by living water (Jeremiah 17:8).
Say aloud or silently:
"I am rooted in Christ. I will not be shaken."

With each breath, feel yourself drawing strength not from striving, but from stillness.
Close with a simple prayer:
"Grow me in Your grace, Lord. Anchor me in Your peace."

Movement-Based Practice: Rhythm Walk

Setup:
Take a slow walk outside if possible, or even inside.

Practice:
Walk without rushing.
With each step, breathe in and out deeply, matching your pace to your breath.

With each step, pray:
 "I move with You, not ahead of You."
 "I move with grace, not grind."

Let the movement reset your nervous system toward rhythms of peace.

Chapter 18: Living Well, Living Whole

> *"This is what the Sovereign Lord, the Holy One of Israel, says: 'In repentance and rest is your salvation, in quietness and trust is your strength, but you would have none of it.'"*- Isaiah 30:15

The Beloved Speaks
"I never imagined I could feel this free. Not just physically, but emotionally. Spiritually. I used to live disconnected. I didn't know but now I know I was performing in church, hiding in my body, chasing health but never feeling whole. This journey brought me back to myself. It brought me home to God. I don't do things perfectly, but I do them with love now. And I know that I am fully seen, fully known, and fully loved. That's what it means to live whole."
— The Beloved

This journey was never meant to be about perfection. Perfectionism, as tempting as it seems, is often a carefully disguised distraction. An enemy-crafted counterfeit that keeps us hustling for worth in all the wrong places. While we chase flawlessness, we miss the invitation to abide. The truth is, perfection is unattainable this side of heaven and God never asked us for it. He asked for presence. From the beginning, He has longed not for your polished performance, but for your surrendered nearness.

The Cross silences the lie that we have to earn our belonging. Performance-based spirituality denies the finished work of Christ. We don't work for love we work from it. Grace is the atmosphere of the Kingdom. And neuroscience confirms what the gospel already taught us: chronic striving, shame, and self-criticism activate stress responses in the brain, hijacking our capacity for connection, clarity, and calm. But when we experience safety in relationship especially with God our parasympathetic nervous system comes online. This is where healing begins: not in the frenzy of fixing, but in the stillness of being fully known and still fully loved.

It was always about peace. Peace that stills the soul and anchors the body. The torment of shame and the whirlwind of self-rejection are schemes of the enemy. But Jesus, the Prince of Peace, desires to dwell with you in goodness and love even in your flesh. Even in the body you've spent years battling. He invites you to honor the skin you're in not because it's flawless, but because it's sacred. Because He knit you together, called it good, and now calls you His.

And now, Beloved, you stand in a new place. Not because your life has become tidy or trouble-free, but because your foundation has shifted. You are no longer a woman striving to fix herself. You are learning to live rooted in a deeper truth: you are the Embodied Beloved. Fully present. Fully loved. And being made whole, from the inside out.

Selah Moment: Breath Prayer

Inhale: I am not behind.
Exhale: I am becoming

Living Well Is More Than "Healthy"

You don't live well just because you count calories, close your rings, or check off your habits in a planner. Health metrics can measure behavior, but they cannot measure embodiment. You can track every step and still be disconnected from the path God has laid before you. You can master a routine and still miss renewal. Because true wellness isn't about performance. It's about presence.

Living well means living *whole*. It means your habits are holy, not just disciplined, but devoted. Your thoughts are no longer running on autopilot but renewed daily by the truth of God's Word (Romans 12:2). Your body is not just conditioned for output but honored as a temple (1 Corinthians 6:19–20). Your soul is not running on empty but nourished in communion with the One who made you. And your joy perhaps long buried beneath busyness or burnout is restored.

This is not another plan to perfect. It's a posture of grace. It's not hustle. It's not hiding. It's not the exhausting cycle of striving, crashing, and starting over. It's a sacred shift into sustainable, Spirit-led living. A life where your worth is not proven through wellness it is *revealed* through wholeness.

Scripture affirms this in the words of the apostle John: *"Beloved, I pray that you may prosper in all things and be in health, just as your soul prospers"* (3 John 1:2, NKJV).

You were never meant to pursue health apart from soul care. Because when your soul is prospering, your body begins to follow. Not perfectly, but peacefully. Not instantly, but sustainably.

Here are 5 embodied practices to begin living well from the inside out:

1. Examine the why behind your habits.
Ask: *Am I doing this out of fear or freedom? Control or communion?*
Track your motivations—not just your macros. Invite the Holy Spirit to reveal where your routines are rooted in striving rather than surrender.

2. Anchor your health rhythms in Scripture and prayer.
Start your morning not with a to-do list, but with truth. Try meditating on one verse as you stretch, breathe, or walk. Let your movement be worship. Let your food choices be led by gratitude, not guilt.

3. Create margin for joy and restoration.
Laughter, sleep, beauty, and stillness are not luxuries they're lifelines. Chronic stress elevates cortisol, compromises immunity, and accelerates aging (McEwen, 2007). Joy is a form of resistance and rest is a weapon against burnout.

4. Practice body blessing over body shaming.
Every time you're tempted to criticize your reflection, pause. Place your hand on your heart and speak this blessing: *"This body is the home God chose for me. I honor it with love, care, and truth."*
Neuroscience confirms that consistent positive self-talk builds new neural pathways toward acceptance and self-compassion.

5. Let your wellness be a witness.
You don't steward your body to impress others you do it to embody the gospel. When you live well, rooted in peace, joy,

and self-control, your life becomes a testimony of God's goodness. Health becomes holy ground.

Remember:

Let this be the part you underline.
The part you circle.
The part you come back to when you're weary, wondering if all this soul work is worth it.

Wellness without wholeness will always leave you empty.
You can eat clean, move daily, and still feel hollow inside.
Because God never asked you to *just* be healthy.
He invites you to be *whole*.

Wholeness is not the absence of struggle.
It's the presence of Christ in the midst of it.
It's choosing grace over grind.
Peace over pressure.
Abiding over achievement.

When your soul is nourished, your body begins to respond not out of fear, but from a place of safety and love.
Not overnight.
Not without resistance.
But with deep, holy steadiness.

Start here:

- Bless your body before you try to change it.

- Nourish your spirit before you numb your symptoms.

- Anchor your habits to heaven, not hustle.

- Let your rhythms be led by love, not lack.

You are the embodied beloved.
And living well isn't about fixing yourself.
It's about returning to the truth:
You were *never* broken beyond repair.
You were *always* worthy of sacred care.

Dog-ear this page.
Come back to it.
Live it.

Wholeness isn't a point you arrive at. It's not the final box checked on your healing journey or the last step in your wellness routine. Wholeness is not linear. It's cyclical, sacred, and Spirit-led. It's not a finish line you cross with your arms raised; it's a rhythm you return to. A flow you learn to live in.

Some days, you'll feel deeply aligned. Your mind clear, your breath steady, your choices flowing from peace and not pressure. You'll feel connected to your body and anchored in the Spirit. And other days? You'll forget. You'll feel off-center. You'll question what you know. But here's the difference: now you know how to return.

Because healing isn't about perfection it's about return.
You've learned where home is.
You've learned that wellness rooted in striving will always burn you out, but wellness rooted in love will keep you grounded.

Whole living is not about always getting it "right."
It's about returning again and again to what is true:

- Rest over rush
- Grace over grind
- Nourishment over neglect
- The Spirit over shame

This is not about trying harder.
This is about *staying close*.
You're not hustling to "get it together" anymore.
You're learning to stay *together* with God.
To walk with Him moment by moment.
To live from union, not urgency.

You are the Embodied Beloved.
That's not a title you earned.
It's an identity you received when you surrendered.

You laid down the hustle.
You broke agreement with shame.
You chose presence over punishment.
You stopped measuring your worth by how many calories you burned or how perfectly you performed.
And now, you move differently.
You nourish differently.
You speak to yourself with compassion instead of criticism.
You rest not out of weakness, but as a form of worship.

Most importantly, you *believe* differently.
And that belief that renewal of the mind is where transformation begins.

"Do not conform to the pattern of this world, but be transformed by the renewing of your mind."
(Romans 12:2, NIV)

Your healing didn't begin when your body changed.
It began when your beliefs did.
Because sustainable change doesn't come from willpower. It flows from identity.

Practical Steps for Living Whole Daily:

1. Morning Check-In:
   Before the world can define your day, align with God. Place your hand on your heart and ask, *"Holy Spirit, where are You moving today, and how can I join You?"*

2. Movement as Worship:
   Whether it's walking, stretching, or lifting connect breath to gratitude.
   Let each step, each rep, each inhale be an embodied prayer.

3. Nourishment Over Numbers:
   Eat to bless, not to control.
   Before each meal, pause and pray: *"Lord, let this food fuel not just my body but my purpose."*

4. Midday Pause for Return:
   When you feel scattered or striving, stop.
   Put both feet on the floor, take three deep breaths, and whisper: *"I return to You, my peace."*

5. Evening Reflection:
   Ask: *Where did I live as the Beloved today?*
   Celebrate the smallest yes. Offer grace for where you forgot. End with this breath prayer: *"You held me today. You'll hold me tomorrow."*

This is whole living.
Not because you've reached perfection
but because you've chosen *presence*.
Not because your life is flawless
but because your *foundation* is faith.

You are not what the world says.
You are not what your past says.
You are not even what your feelings say.

You are the Embodied Beloved.
And that belief changes *everything*.

Reflection Prompts

1. What does "living well" mean to you now, after this journey?

2. Where do you feel most free in your wellness rhythms? Where are you still learning?

3. How can you return to wholeness when life gets messy or hard?

4. What has God taught you about your body, your story, and your belovedness?

Embodied Prayer

Father,
Thank You for walking with me every step of this journey.
Thank You for calling me to more, not through striving, but through surrender.
I am no longer chasing perfection. I am choosing presence.
I am no longer disconnected from my body. I am dwelling in the temple You gave me.
Help me walk forward in grace.
Let my life reflect my wholeness.
Let my habits reflect Your holiness.
Let everything I do be rooted in the truth:
I am the Beloved. And I am learning to live like it.
In Jesus' name, Amen.

Covered & Held Stillness Practice

Setup:
Lie down or sit upright with one hand over your belly, the other over your heart. Close your eyes.

Practice: Breathe in deeply. Let your breath drop into your belly.
As you inhale, say: "I am whole."
As you exhale, say:
"I am held."

Stay here for a few minutes. Let this truth settle deeper than your striving.
You don't have to *become* whole.
You already *are* in Him.

Movement-Based Practice
The Wholeness Walk

Setup:
Take a 10-minute walk, outside if possible, or around your space.

Practice:
As you move, say aloud or silently:
"With each step, I return to wholeness."
"With each breath, I walk in freedom."

Let this be a walk of *integration*—where what you believe in your heart meets what your body remembers.

Ready to put what you've read into practice?
Download the FaithFueled Life App and take your journey deeper. Inside, you'll find guided breath prayers, embodied movement sessions, Scripture meditations, and soul-strengthening practices that bring this book to life. Whether you're seeking stillness, strength, or spiritual renewal, the app gives you real-time tools to embody your faith and steward your temple; anytime, anywhere.

Don't just read about transformation. Live it.
www.tinyurl.com/FAITHFUELEDAPP and begin your journey of becoming the Embodied Beloved.

Chapter 19: Making Disciples with Your Story

This is to my Father's glory, that you bear much fruit, showing yourselves to be my disciples.-John 15:8

The Beloved Speaks

> *"I didn't get here by chasing perfection. I got here by choosing presence. My healing became real when I stopped hiding my story and started living it out loud. That's when everything changed. When my focus went from serving myself to serving others the divine opportunities God opened up to be useful to serve the kingdom were immeasurably more than I could ask or imagine and what once was a vain pursuit to become skinny became a purpose and calling to help women embody they are beloved"*
> — De

Ten years ago, I was 100 pounds heavier, carrying not just weight in my body but weight in my soul. My body was aching, inflamed, and exhausted. But more than that, I was numb emotionally, spiritually, and physically disconnected from myself and from God. I was a church-going woman with a fractured sense of identity, living by the lie that if I just tried harder, performed better, or shrank smaller, I'd finally be worthy of love.

But the truth? I was already loved. I just didn't know how to receive it.

This is the soil where God began to till the ground of my heart. I didn't wake up one day "healed." I woke up one day *hungry*. Not just for food. but for freedom. And in that hunger, God met me. He invited me not into another weight loss program, but into a relationship where I would discover that the most radical transformation isn't just physical, it's spiritual, mental, and emotional. That kind of healing doesn't just change your habits; it changes your harvest. I can honestly say that because I am living testimony. I have walked it and I now I teach others how to overcome.

Because here's what I've learned: when God heals you, He doesn't stop with you. He intends to multiply that healing in others.

Jesus said, "By this My Father is glorified, that you bear much fruit and so prove to be My disciples" (John 15:8). The fruit isn't just for our benefit. It's to nourish others. Our stories especially the raw, unfinished ones become fertile ground for discipleship when we stop hiding them and start sowing them.

The world tells us to lead from perfection. Jesus tells us to lead from *redemption.*

I didn't lose 100 pounds because I found a miracle pill or a quick fix. I lost it because I surrendered not just food, but control. I stopped worshiping my willpower and started walking with the Holy Spirit. I began to listen to my body instead of shame it. I stopped treating exercise like punishment and started moving in joy. I nourished myself not just with food, but with truth. And I invited Jesus into every part of the journey, especially the messy, inconsistent parts I used to keep hidden.

It wasn't about striving. It was about abiding.

And the fruit of that transformation? It now feeds others. Through my coaching, classes, speaking, and writing, I've watched other women begin to believe again not in diets or discipline, but in the God who restores.

Selah Moment: Breath Prayer

Inhale: *My story is seed.*
Exhale: *May it bear fruit for Your glory.*
Breathe with intention. Receive the truth that you don't need to be finished to be faithful. Let each exhale release fear of being "too much" or "not enough." You are not performing you are planting.

Science calls this "post-traumatic growth" the phenomenon where individuals who endure significant struggle don't just return to baseline they flourish. Neurologically, healing doesn't just restore brain pathways; it creates new ones. Spiritually, God doesn't just bring us back to where we were. He resurrects us into something we've never been.

Your story is not just about where you've been. It's about where you're going and who gets to come with you.

We often disqualify ourselves because we still feel unfinished. But let me tell you: God does not wait for perfect people to carry His message. He chose a woman at a well with a past (John 4), a demon-possessed man in a graveyard (Mark 5), and a hot-headed fisherman with impulse control (Peter!).

He's not after polish. He's after people willing to tell the truth and point to the Healer.

Discipleship isn't about having all the answers. It's about having a testimony that points to the Answer. When you share your story your whole story you give others permission to hope again. When you lead with vulnerability instead of victory, people can see themselves in you. And when they see transformation in you, they begin to believe it's possible for them.

That's how healing becomes a harvest.

And not just any harvest a generational one. What you break off in your lifetime can become freedom for your children, your community, and women you may never meet. The trauma you've metabolized, the lies you've renounced, the embodiment you've reclaimed all of it becomes seed.

So tell your story.
Tell it before it's perfect.
Tell it before you've "arrived."
Tell it while the soil is still tender and the sprouts are still fragile.

Because someone is standing in a field of despair, waiting for a glimpse of fruit. You are the Embodied Beloved. And your healing is not just for you. It's for the world God has called you to nourish. Let your story multiply.

Reflection Prompts

1. What part of your story have you been afraid to share?
   What holds you back from telling the truth of your healing?

2. Who is already eating from the fruit of your transformation whether you've realized it or not?
   Think of a conversation, compliment, or moment that revealed your growth was nourishing someone else.

3. What do you still believe disqualifies you from making disciples?
   Bring that belief into the light and replace it with a truth from Scripture.

4. How would your story shift if you viewed your healing as a harvest, not just a testimony?
   What fruit do you hope to see multiply in the lives of others?

5. Who is your "one"?
   Who is one person you could mentor, encourage, or walk with as they begin their own journey toward wholeness?

Embodied Prayer

Jesus,
You didn't just save me. You are still saving me. Still healing. Still growing me.
Thank You for not wasting a single part of my story.
Not the pain, not the process, not even the parts I wanted to

hide.
Make my life a living seed, God. Use what You've restored in me to restore others.
I don't want to just be free. I want to lead others into freedom.
So here I am. Use me, unfinished and fully Yours.
Let my healing become a harvest.
Amen.

Covered & Held: Stillness Practice

Rooted in Testimony, Reaching for Multiplication

1. Lie on your back, knees bent, feet planted.
   Let your spine feel supported by the ground beneath you. Arms open in surrender.

2. Breathe deeply, repeating silently:
   "You've brought me through." (Inhale)
   "Now bring fruit from it." (Exhale)

3. Place one hand on your belly, one on your heart.
   Feel the story you've carried. Feel the life growing from it.

4. Visualize your story as a seed.
   Planted in God's soil. Watered by His mercy. Growing not for your glory, but for His kingdom.

5. Rest.
   Let your nervous system memorize what it feels like to be safe in your story.

Movement Practice

Sow & Stretch: Moving with Testimony

This 15-minute flow moves through grounded postures that symbolize surrender, seed, and harvest.

1. Prayer Pose
Begin in surrender. Breathe into your back. Let go of shame.

2. Tabletop to Pike
Flow gently. Think: "From my knees to my calling."

3. Overhead Lunge with Open Arms
Lift your chest, reach wide. Declare openness to lead with your story.

4. Low Squat
A seed posture. Stay low. Stay grounded. Breathe into the hips; your power center.

5. Power Pose
Stand tall, arms open wide. Shine. Expand. Offer.

6. Resting Pose
Receive. Let the Spirit speak. Let your breath remind you that you're already enough.

Chapter 20: This Is My Body Story: From Orphan Spirit to Embodied Beloved

He lifted me out of the slimy pit, out of the mud and mire; he set my feet on a rock and gave me a firm place to stand. He put a new song in my mouth, a hymn of praise to our God. Many will see and fear the Lord and put their trust in him.-
Psalm 40:2-3

I didn't always love my body.

In fact, for most of my life, I treated it like a burden, a battleground, or something to be ignored.
Never a blessing.

I didn't always know God as Father.
I knew Him as authority. Distant. A rule-maker.
Someone I was trying to impress with good behavior and quiet suffering.

For most of my life, I was disconnected from my body, my worth, and what love was supposed to feel like.
Not just physically, but spiritually, emotionally, and generationally.

Not because I wanted to be, but because of the story I was born into.

My mother was there physically but not emotionally.
Addiction took her from me in a thousand subtle ways.
She chose everything and everyone but me.

I learned early that I had to raise myself.
And now, even as a grown woman with a husband and children of my own,
I'm still raising her ,too.

My father disowned me when I was 19.
That door closed and never reopened.
I'm 42 now, and he still hasn't met his grandchildren.

I've spent most of my life battling a deep, unspoken belief that I was never wanted.
That I had to earn love. Prove my worth. Stay small. Make myself useful to belong.

I wasn't an orphan by circumstance.
But I carried an orphan spirit.
And it shaped everything especially how I saw my body.

My ACE (Adverse Childhood Experiences) score is 8.
That number doesn't define me, but it does tell you something:

I was shaped by trauma.
I learned early that rejection could come at any time.
That love might leave.
That to be safe, I had to be small, invisible, and pleasing.

And I carried those beliefs into adulthood… and into my body.

I lived most of my life as a high-functioning orphan.
I looked like I had it together.
I smiled. I served.

But on the inside, I was disconnected from people, from safety, from my own body.

I turned to outside comforts to quiet the discomfort inside.
What I could control became my trap: substances, food, people.
I didn't realize I was feeding my soul with things that couldn't satisfy.

I didn't trust my body.
I fed it to numb myself.
I punished it to try to feel worthy.
I ignored it when it cried out for care.

At my heaviest, I weighed 236 pounds.
But the heaviest thing I carried wasn't weight. It was worthlessness.
The belief that my body was something I had to fix.
That *who I was* was a flaw.
Always flawed. Constantly pointed out.

I didn't need a new diet.
I needed a new identity.

And I didn't find it in a gym or on a scale.
I found it in Jesus.

I left the church for years.
It was just another standard I couldn't live up to.
Another place to be rejected for who I was.
Another Father I lacked approval from.

I didn't fear God in reverence.
I feared Him like I feared every man who left.
Distant. Disappointed. Done with me.

I thought no matter how hard I tried, I'd never be worthy.

Then one day on yet another attempt to shrink what I saw in the mirror, I started another diet.
I thought I was chasing weight loss.
But God was chasing me.

That desire to get skinny revealed how spiritually underweight I really was.
And the physical weight I tried to carry alone led me right into the arms of the Father I'd been running from.

Over time, I lost more than 100 pounds.
 But what I really lost were the lies:

That I was unlovable.
That I had to earn everything including healing.
That I was too broken to be used by God.

And what I gained?

Wholeness.
Peace in my skin.
The joy of moving my body in worship.
Purpose.
The revelation that I am *not* an orphan.

I am the **Embodied Beloved.**

My breaking point wasn't loud.
It wasn't one big "aha" moment.

It was a slow undoing.
A gentle invitation from God I almost didn't hear.

He didn't meet me with shame.
He met me with presence.

Not once did God say, *"Hurry up and get it together."*
He said, *"Come. You're already Mine."*

One step at a time, I said yes.

To walking.
To nourishing.
To moving in worship.
To believing I could be well not just thinner, but whole.

And as I shed the weight, I started shedding the lies:

I am not abandoned.
I am not too much.
I am not a mistake.
I am the Embodied Beloved.

He didn't shout. He whispered:

> *"Daughter, I never left. I've always loved you body and all.*
> *Let Me show you who you really are."*

So I began to say yes.
One walk at a time. One meal at a time. One prayer at a time.

It was messy.
I cried. I fell. I wrestled. I restarted.

But I kept going. Because God wasn't done with me yet.

This is why I wrote this book.

Not because I have it all figured out.
But because I've walked through the fire and I'm still here.
Still healing. Still testifying.

If you've ever felt like your body is too far gone...
If you've believed your story disqualifies you...
If you've wrestled with shame so heavy it felt holy

This book is for you.

I want to see you free.
I want to see you nourished.
I want to see you live as the Embodied Beloved not just in your spirit, but in your habits, your healing, and your whole life.

You are not too much.
You are not too far gone.
And you are not alone.

If you've carried rejection like a second skin...
If your body has been the place where grief lives...
If you've been waiting until you "get it together" to finally feel worthy

I want you to know:

You are already loved.
And you are already welcome.

Embodied Blessing

Beloved,
You are not what happened to you.
You are not the weight you carry on your body or in your heart.
You are not defined by the people who walked away.

You are loved. Seen. Known. Called.

Your body is holy ground.
Your story is not too messy for God.
He will use every part of it, *especially* the broken parts, to bring freedom to others.

Let Him.

Because He's already chosen you.
Now it's your turn to live like it.

Epilogue: To the One Who Made It to the End

Beloved,

If you're reading this, I want you to know. I see you.
Not with my eyes, but with my heart. With my memory. With my testimony.
Because I know what it takes to get here.

It takes courage to stay.
To turn the page when it hurts.
To keep reading when the lies start yelling.
To choose hope when shame wants to keep you silent.

You've done that.

You've journeyed through every chapter.
You've sat with your story.
You've invited God into your body, your beliefs, your breath.
And whether you feel like it or not, *you are already transforming.*

I didn't write this book as an expert.
I wrote it as a woman who's been buried and brought back to life.
Who's known the ache of abandonment, the grip of shame, the quiet desperation to be whole.
I wrote this for the woman who thinks she's too far gone or too broken to begin again.

I wrote this for *you.*

And I want you to remember something:

You are not behind.
You are not disqualified.
You are not too much.
You are not alone.

You are a daughter of the King.
You are deeply loved.
You are a temple.
You are the embodied beloved.

And you do not have to wait for another Monday, another miracle, or another milestone to live like it.

Start now.

A Breath of Blessing

May your habits be holy, not heavy.
May your movement be worship, not punishment.
May your food be freedom, not fear.
May your mind be renewed daily.
May your soul be nourished deeply.
May your breath be slow and full of grace.

May your body become your sanctuary.
Not perfect. Not polished. But peaceful. Present. Whole.

And may you always remember:
You do not need to chase worthiness.
You already have it.
You are already His.

And He is not just transforming your life
He's *transfiguring* it.

From ashes to beauty.
From striving to surrender.
From orphan to embodied beloved.

Walk in it.

With you,
De Bolton

A Blessing Over Your Becoming

Beloved,
You have journeyed far.
You have touched the hem of healing.
You have opened pages you were afraid to open
Pages in your story, pages in your soul.
And still… you came.
Still… you stayed.
Still… you rose.

Now, may you rise every day like this:
Not reaching for perfection,
But rooted in presence.
Not hiding your pain,
But honoring your healing.

May the lies fall silent.
May the striving cease.
May the temple of your body be filled with peace.

When you forget who you are,
Return to the mirror of this truth:
You are the one Jesus loves.
You are the one He died for.
You are the one He chose to dwell in.

And you are not just walking away with information.
You are walking away with transformation.

So take this wholeness and wear it like a mantle.
Take your story and carry it like a lantern.

Take your breath, your body, your becoming, and live it like worship.

The world needs what God is doing in you.
The world needs what God is doing through you.

Go now in the name of the One who made you whole:
Jesus; the Healer, the Shepherd, the Beloved who first called you His own.

Amen.

References

Chapter 1: You Are the Beloved
Leaf, C. (2013). Switch on your brain: The key to peak happiness, thinking, and health. Baker Books.

Price, C. J., & Hooven, C. (2018). Interoceptive awareness skills for emotion regulation: Theory and approach of Mindful Awareness in Body-oriented Therapy (MABT). Frontiers in Psychology, 9, 798. https://doi.org/10.3389/fpsyg.2018.00798

van der Kolk, B. (2014). The body keeps the score: Brain, mind, and body in the healing of trauma. Penguin Books.

Chapter 2: Grace Over Grind
McEwen, B. S. (2006). *The impact of stress on the human body: Insights from studies of allostatic load.* Annals of the New York Academy of Sciences, 1094(1), 1–15. https://doi.org/10.1196/annals.1376.001

Sapolsky, R. M. (2004). *Why zebras don't get ulcers: The acclaimed guide to stress, stress-related diseases, and coping* (3rd ed.). Henry Holt and Company.

Thompson, C. (2015). *The soul of shame: Retelling the stories we believe about ourselves.* InterVarsity Press.

Tindle, H. A., Davis, R. B., Phillips, R. S., & Eisenberg, D. M. (2005). Trends in use of spiritual healing techniques in the United States: 1990–2001. *Alternative Therapies in Health and Medicine*, 11(1), 42–49.

Willard, D. (2006). *The great omission: Reclaiming Jesus's essential teachings on discipleship.* HarperOne.

Chapter 3: Your Body Is a Temple
Leaf, C. (2013). Switch on your brain: The key to peak happiness, thinking, and health. Baker Books.

Doidge, N. (2007). The brain that changes itself: Stories of personal triumph from the frontiers of brain science. Viking.

Newberg, A., & Waldman, M. R. (2009). How God changes your brain: Breakthrough findings from a leading neuroscientist. Ballantine Books.

van der Kolk, B. A. (2014). The body keeps the score: Brain, mind, and body in the healing of trauma. Viking.

Scaer, R. C. (2005). The trauma spectrum: Hidden wounds and human resiliency. W.W. Norton & Company.

Worthington, E. L. Jr. (2006). Forgiveness and reconciliation: Theory and application. Routledge.

Koenig, H. G. (2005). Faith and mental health: Religious resources for healing. Templeton Foundation Press.

Feinberg, M. (2016). Proven: Stop striving, start resting. B&H Publishing.

Chapter 4: Releasing False Scenarions

Leaf, C. (2013). *Switch on your brain: The key to peak happiness, thinking, and health.* Baker Books.

van der Kolk, B. (2014). *The body keeps the score: Brain, mind, and body in the healing of trauma.* Penguin Books.

Worthington, E. L., & Scherer, M. (2004). Forgiveness is an emotion-focused coping strategy that can reduce health risks and promote health resilience. *Psychology & Health, 19*(3), 385–405. https://doi.org/10.1080/0887044042000196674

Toussaint, L. L., Owen, A. D., & Cheadle, A. (2016). Forgive to live: Forgiveness, health, and longevity. *Journal of Behavioral Medicine, 39*(2), 229–238. https://doi.org/10.1007/s10865-015-9672-2

Chapter 5: Forgiveness: The Doorway to Wholeness

Mayer, E. A., Knight, R., Mazmanian, S. K., Cryan, J. F., & Tillisch, K. (2015). Gut microbes and the brain: Paradigm shift in neuroscience. *Journal of Neuroscience, 34*(46),

15490–15496.
Leaf, C. (2013). *Switch on your brain: The key to peak happiness, thinking, and health.* Baker Books.
Tomiyama, A. J., Dallman, M. F., & Epel, E. S. (2011). *Comfort food is comforting to those most stressed: Evidence of the chronic stress response network in high stress women. Psychoneuroendocrinology, 36*(10), 1513–1519. https://doi.org/10.1016/j.psyneuen.2011.04.005
Mayer, E. A., Knight, R., Mazmanian, S. K., Cryan, J. F., & Tillisch, K. (2015). *Gut microbes and the brain: Paradigm shift in neuroscience. Journal of Neuroscience, 35*(46), 13884–13893. https://doi.org/10.1523/JNEUROSCI.2912-15.2015

Chapter 6: Living a Mindset of Freedom
Doidge, N. (2007). *The brain that changes itself: Stories of personal triumph from the frontiers of brain science.* Penguin Books.
Luders, E., Toga, A. W., Lepore, N., & Gaser, C. (2009). The underlying anatomical correlates of long-term meditation: Larger hippocampal and frontal volumes of gray matter. *NeuroImage, 45*(3), 672–678.

Chapter 7:The Gut-Heart-Brain Connection
Mayer, E. A. (2011). *The Mind-Gut Connection: How the Hidden Conversation Within Our Bodies Impacts Our Mood, Our Choices, and Our Overall Health.* Harper Wave.
Porges, S. W. (2011). *The polyvagal theory: Neurophysiological foundations of emotions, attachment, communication, and self-regulation.* W. W. Norton & Company.
McCraty, R., & Zayas, M. A. (2014). Cardiac coherence, self-regulation, autonomic stability, and psychosocial well-being. *Frontiers in Psychology, 5,* 1090.

https://doi.org/10.3389/fpsyg.2014.01090
Gershon, M. D. (1998). *The Second Brain: A Groundbreaking New Understanding of Nervous Disorders of the Stomach and Intestine.* Harper Perennial.
Sapolsky, R. M. (2004). *Why Zebras Don't Get Ulcers: The Acclaimed Guide to Stress, Stress-Related Diseases, and Coping.* Holt Paperbacks.
Endocrine Society. (2016). *Endocrine Facts and Figures: Stress and the HPA Axis.*
https://www.endocrine.org
van der Kolk, B. A. (2014). *The Body Keeps the Score: Brain, Mind, and Body in the Healing of Trauma.* Viking.
Thompson, R. F., & Spencer, W. A. (1966). Habituation: A model phenomenon for the study of neuronal substrates of behavior. *Psychological Review, 73*(1), 16–43.
Craig, A. D. (2002). How do you feel? Interoception: the sense of the physiological condition of the body. *Nature Reviews Neuroscience, 3*(8), 655–666. https://doi.org/10.1038/nrn894
Northoff, G., & Panksepp, J. (2008). The trans-species concept of self and the subcortical–cortical midline system. *Trends in Cognitive Sciences, 12*(7), 259–264.

Chapter 8: Reclaiming Movement as a Spiritual Act
Fox, G. R., Kaplan, J., Damasio, H., & Damasio, A. (2015). Neural correlates of gratitude. *Frontiers in Psychology, 6,* 1491. https://doi.org/10.3389/fpsyg.2015.01491
Endocrine Society. (2016). Adrenal fatigue is not a real medical condition. Retrieved from https://www.endocrine.org/news-and-advocacy/news-room/2016/adrenal-fatigue-is-not-a-real-medical-condition
Hackney, A. C. (2006). Stress and the neuroendocrine system: the role of exercise as a stressor and modifier of

stress. Expert Review of Endocrinology & Metabolism, 1(6), 783–792. https://doi.org/10.1586/17446651.1.6.783

Ratey, J. J. (2008). Spark: The Revolutionary New Science of Exercise and the Brain. Little, Brown Spark.

Porges, S. W. (2011). *The polyvagal theory: Neurophysiological foundations of emotions, attachment, communication, and self-regulation.* W.W. Norton & Company.

Ratey, J. J. (2008). *Spark: The revolutionary new science of exercise and the brain.* Little, Brown Spark.

van der Kolk, B. A. (2014). *The body keeps the score: Brain, mind, and body in the healing of trauma.* Penguin Books.

Chapter 9: Sustainable Fitness for Your Season

Cavill, N., Kahlmeier, S., & Racioppi, F. (2006). *Physical activity and health in Europe: Evidence for action.* WHO.

Mehling, W. E., Wrubel, J., Daubenmier, J. J., Price, C. J., Kerr, C. E., Silow, T., & Stewart, A. L. (2011). Body awareness: a phenomenological inquiry into the common ground of mind-body therapies. *Philosophy, Ethics, and Humanities in Medicine*, 6(1), 1-12.

Semenchuk, B. N., Strachan, S. M., & Fortier, M. (2018). Self-compassion and the self-regulation of exercise: Reactions to recalled exercise setbacks. *Journal of Sport and Exercise Psychology*, 40(1), 31–39.

Ratey, J. J. (2008). Spark: The revolutionary new science of exercise and the brain. Little, Brown.

Porges, S. W. (2011). The polyvagal theory: Neurophysiological foundations of emotions, attachment, communication, and self-regulation. W. W. Norton & Company

Cavill, N., Biddle, S., & Sallis, J. F. (2006). Health enhancing physical activity for young people: Statement of the United Kingdom expert consensus conference. Pediatric Exercise Science, 13(1), 12–25.

Semenchuk, B. N., Strachan, S. M., & Fortier, M. (2018). Self-compassion and the self-regulation of exercise: Reactions to recalled exercise setbacks. Journal of Sport and Exercise Psychology, 40(1), 31–39. https://doi.org/10.1123/jsep.2017-0156

Mehling, W. E., Wrubel, J., Daubenmier, J. J., Price, C. J., Kerr, C. E., Silow, T., ... & Stewart, A. L. (2011). Body awareness: A phenomenological inquiry into the common ground of mind-body therapies. Philosophy, Ethics, and Humanities in Medicine, 6(1), 6. https://doi.org/10.1186/1747-5341-6-6

Chapter 10: From Body Battle to Body Blessing

Falk, E. B. (2014). Changing behavior with neuroimaging. The New York Times.

Kemeny, M. E. (2003). The psychobiology of stress. Current Directions in Psychological Science, 12(4), 124–129. https://doi.org/10.1111/1467-8721.01246

Porges, S. W. (2011). The polyvagal theory: Neurophysiological foundations of emotions, attachment, communication, and self-regulation. W. W. Norton & Company.

Ratey, J. J. (2008). Spark: The revolutionary new science of exercise and the brain. Little, Brown Spark.

Van der Kolk, B. A. (2014). The body keeps the score: Brain, mind, and body in the healing of trauma. Penguin Books.

Chapter 11: What Do I Do to Move? How Much? How Long? Why?

American College of Sports Medicine. (2009). ACSM's guidelines for exercise testing and prescription (8th ed.). Lippincott Williams & Wilkins.

Williams, C. (2021). Move: How the new science of body movement can set your mind free. Profile Books.

Wilmore, J. H., Costill, D. L., & Kenney, W. L. (2008). Physiology of sport and exercise (4th ed.). Human Kinetics.

Porges, S. W. (2011). The polyvagal theory: Neurophysiological foundations of emotions, attachment, communication, and self-regulation. W. W. Norton & Company.

World Health Organization. (2020). WHO guidelines on physical activity and sedentary behaviour. https://www.who.int/publications/i/item/9789240015128

McGonigal, K. (2015). The Joy of Movement: How Exercise Helps Us Find Happiness, Hope, Connection, and Courage. Avery.

Centers for Disease Control and Prevention. (2022). Physical activity basics. https://www.cdc.gov/physicalactivity/basics/index.htm

Hillman, C. H., Erickson, K. I., & Kramer, A. F. (2008). Be smart, exercise your heart: Exercise effects on brain and cognition. Nature Reviews Neuroscience, 9(1), 58–65. https://doi.org/10.1038/nrn2298

Chapter 12: Nourish to Flourish

Barna Group. (2020). *State of the Church: Trends in American Christianity*.

Bruce, L. J., & Ricciardelli, L. A. (2016). A systematic review of the psychosocial correlates of intuitive eating among adult women. *Appetite, 96*, 454–472.

Tylka, T. L., & Kroon Van Diest, A. M. (2013). The Intuitive Eating Scale–2: Assessment of reliability and construct validity. *Journal of Counseling Psychology, 60*(1), 137–153.

Wansink, B. (2010). *Mindless eating: Why we eat more than we think*. Bantam.

Leaf, C. (2013). *Switch on your brain: The key to peak happiness, thinking, and health*. Baker Books.

Chapter 13: Fed by Grace, Not by Guilt
Porges, S. W. (2011). *The polyvagal theory: Neurophysiological foundations of emotions, attachment, communication, and self-regulation.* W. W. Norton & Company.
Sapolsky, R. M. (2004). *Why zebras don't get ulcers: The acclaimed guide to stress, stress-related diseases, and coping.* Henry Holt and Company.
Siegel, D. J. (2012). *The developing mind: How relationships and the brain interact to shape who we are* (2nd ed.). Guilford Press.
Sutton, E. F., Beyl, R., Early, K. S., Cefalu, W. T., Ravussin, E., & Peterson, C. M. (2018). Early time-restricted feeding improves insulin sensitivity, blood pressure, and oxidative stress even without weight loss in men with prediabetes. *Cell Metabolism, 27*(6), 1212–1221.e3.
https://doi.org/10.1016/j.cmet.2018.04.010
Walker, M. (2017). *Why we sleep: Unlocking the power of sleep and dreams.* Scribner.

Chapter 14: Satisfy and Sustain
McEwen, B. S. (2007). Physiology and neurobiology of stress and adaptation: Central role of the brain. *Physiological Reviews, 87*(3), 873–904.
Porges, S. W. (2011). *The polyvagal theory: Neurophysiological foundations of emotions, attachment, communication, and self-regulation.* W. W. Norton & Company.

Chapter 15: Holy Rhythms and Nourishment
Porges, S. W. (2011). *The polyvagal theory: Neurophysiological foundations of emotions, attachment, communication, and self-regulation.* W. W. Norton & Company.

McEwen, B. S. (2007). Physiology and neurobiology of stress and adaptation: Central role of the brain. *Physiological Reviews, 87*(3), 873–904.

Sutton, E. F., Beyl, R., Early, K. S., Cefalu, W. T., Ravussin, E., & Peterson, C. M. (2018). Early time-restricted feeding improves insulin sensitivity, blood pressure, and oxidative stress even without weight loss in men with prediabetes. *Cell Metabolism, 27*(6), 1212–1221.

Romans 12:2 (NIV). *Do not conform to the pattern of this world, but be transformed by the renewing of your mind.*

3 John 1:2 (NKJV). *Beloved, I pray that you may prosper in all things and be in health, just as your soul prospers.*

Chapter 16: What do I eat? How? Why?

Tylka, T. L., & Kroon Van Diest, A. M. (2013). The Intuitive Eating Scale–2: Item refinement and psychometric evaluation with college women and men. *Journal of Counseling Psychology, 60*(1), 137–153. https://doi.org/10.1037/a0030893

Precision Nutrition. (n.d.). *The complete guide to portion sizes using your hands*. Retrieved June 15, 2025, from https://www.precisionnutrition.com/portion-control-guide

Willett, W. C., Rockström, J., Loken, B., Springmann, M., Lang, T., Vermeulen, S., … & Murray, C. J. L. (2019). Food in the Anthropocene: the EAT–Lancet Commission on healthy diets from sustainable food systems. The Lancet, 393(10170), 447–492. https://doi.org/10.1016/S0140-6736(18)31788-4

Harvard T.H. Chan School of Public Health. (n.d.). The Nutrition Source: Healthy Eating Plate & Pyramid. https://www.hsph.harvard.edu/nutritionsource/

Brown, A. W., Brown, M. M., Allison, D. B. (2013). Belief beyond the evidence: Using the proposed effect of breakfast on obesity to show two practices that distort scientific evidence. The American Journal of Clinical Nutrition, 98(5),

1298–1308. https://doi.org/10.3945/ajcn.113.064410
Albers, S. (2012). Eating mindfully: How to end mindless eating and enjoy a balanced relationship with food (2nd ed.). New Harbinger Publications.
Satter, E. (2007). Secrets of Feeding a Healthy Family: How to Eat, How to Raise Good Eaters, How to Cook. Kelcy Press.
Tribole, E., & Resch, E. (2020). Intuitive Eating: A Revolutionary Anti-Diet Approach (4th ed.). St. Martin's Essentials.
Harvard Medical School. (2021). The gut-brain connection. https://www.health.harvard.edu/diseases-and-conditions/the-gut-brain-connection

Chapter 17: Holy Habits, Not Hustle Routines
lear, J. (2018). *Atomic habits: An easy & proven way to build good habits & break bad ones*. Avery.
Hebb, D. O. (1949). *The organization of behavior: A neuropsychological theory*. Wiley.
McEwen, B. S. (2007). Physiology and neurobiology of stress and adaptation: Central role of the brain. *Physiological Reviews, 87*(3), 873–904. https://doi.org/10.1152/physrev.00041.2006
Porges, S. W. (2011). *The polyvagal theory: Neurophysiological foundations of emotions, attachment, communication, and self-regulation*. W. W. Norton & Company.

Chapter 18: Living Well, Living Whole
McEwen, B. S. (2007). Physiology and neurobiology of stress and adaptation: Central role of the brain. *Physiological Reviews, 87*(3), 873–904. ttps://doi.org/10.1152/physrev.00041.2006

Chapter 19: Making Disciples with your story
Tedeschi, R. G., & Calhoun, L. G. (2004). Posttraumatic growth: Conceptual foundations and empirical evidence. *Psychological Inquiry, 15*(1), 1–18.
https://doi.org/10.1207/s15327965pli1501_01

Scripture References

Chapter 1: Becoming the Beloved
Matthew 3:17
Isaiah 43:1
Psalm 139:13–14
Romans 8:15–16

Chapter 2: Grace Over Grind
Hebrews 4:10
Titus 2:11–12
Matthew 11:28–30

Chapter 3: Your Body Is a Temple
Romans 12:1–2
1 Corinthians 6:19–20
Proverbs 23:7
Philippians 4:8

Chapter 4: Releasing False Scenarios
Colossians 3:13
Matthew 6:14–15
Psalm 103:12
Romans 8:1
1 John 1:9

Chapter 5: Forgiveness: The Doorway to Wholeness
Genesis 3:7–10
Romans 5:20
2 Corinthians 12:9
Isaiah 61:7

Chapter 6: Living a Mindset of Freedom
Revelation 12:11
2 Corinthians 5:17
Romans 5:8
Isaiah 43:18–19

Chapter 7: The Gut-Brain-Heart Connection
Luke 8:48
Psalm 139:13–14
Proverbs 14:30
Proverbs 17:22
Proverbs 18:14
Proverbs 4:23
Philippians 2:1 (KJV)
Philippians 4:7

Chapter 8: Reclaiming Movement as a Spiritual Act
Acts 17:28
1 Corinthians 10:31
Psalm 150:4
Romans 12:1

Chapter 9: Sustainable Fitness for Your Season
Ecclesiastes 3:1
Isaiah 40:31
1 Timothy 4:8

Chapter 10: From Body Battle to Body Blessing
Genesis 1:27
1 Samuel 16:7
1 Corinthians 9:24–27
Romans 8:11

Chapter 11: What do I do to move? How much? How long? Why?
Job 10:8, 11
Genesis 2:15
1 Corinthians 6:19–20
Romans 12:1
Psalm 150:6
Psalm 139:14
1 Corinthians 10:31

Chapter 12:- Nourish to Flourish
1 Corinthians 6:12
Galatians 5:1
John 6:35
Deuteronomy 8:3

Chapter 13: Fed by Grace, Not by guilt
Galatians 5:13
1 Corinthians 6:12
Galatians 5:1
Romans 12:1
Genesis 1:29
Psalm 34:8
1 Corinthians 10:31
Matthew 4:4

Chapter 14: Satisfy and Sustain
Romans 8:14
Galatians 5:22–23
Proverbs 25:16
Acts 2:46

Chapter 15: Holy Rhythms of Nourishment
Exodus 16:4–5
Matthew 6:11
Romans 14:17
Isaiah 55:2

Chapter 16: What do I eat? How? Why?
Genesis 1:29
Genesis 3:1
Psalm 139:14
1 Corinthians 6:19
Jeremiah 17:7–8
Psalm 1:3
Matthew 5:14–16
John 15:5

Chapter 17: Holy Habits, Not Hustle Routines
Matthew 28:19–20
2 Timothy 1:7
Revelation 12:11
Ephesians 2:10

Chapter 18: Living Well, Living Whole
2 Corinthians 10:5
Romans 12:2
John 8:32
Psalm 34:5

Chapter 19: Making Disciples with Your Story
Isaiah 30:15
John 10:10
Romans 8:6
Colossians 3:15–17

Chapter 20: The Embodied Beloved Life
Romans 5:5
Galatians 2:20
1 John 4:12
Philippians 1:6

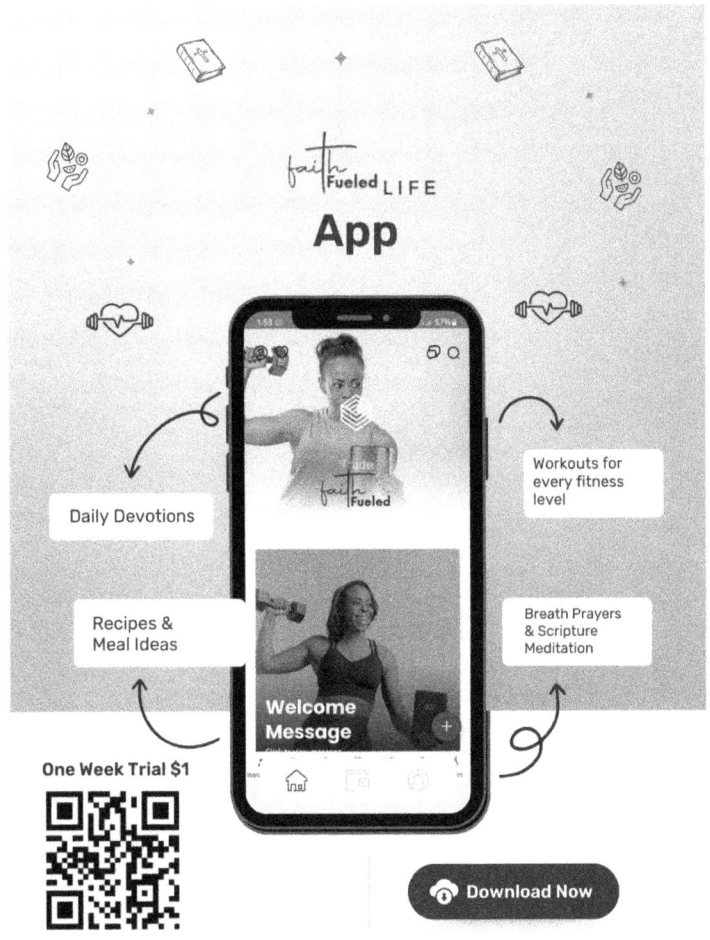

www.ingramcontent.com/pod-product-compliance
Lightning Source LLC
Chambersburg PA
CBHW032150080426
42735CB00008B/653